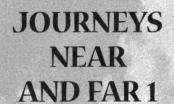

JOURNEYS
NEAR
AND FAR 1

JOURNEYS NEAR AND FAR 1
Reading and Responding Critically

Jessie M. Reppy
Kean University

Linda Best
Kean University

Houghton Mifflin Company
Boston ◆ New York

Director, World Languages: Marketing and ESL Publishing   Susan Maguire
Senior Associate Editor   Kathy Sands Boehmer
Editorial Assistant   Manuel Muñoz
Senior Project Editor   Kathryn Dinovo
Senior Cover Design Coordinator   Deborah Azerrad Savona
Senior Manufacturing Coordinator   Marie Barnes
Marketing Manager   Jay Hu
Marketing Associate   Claudia Martínez

Cover design   Rebecca Fagan
Cover image   Tana Powell

Photo credits   p. 1: © STONE/Howard Grey; © STONE/Zigy Kaluzny; © STONE/Peter
Dokus; © STONE/ Rich Iwasaki. **p. 6:** Ozier Muhammad/New York Times Pictures.
p. 16: © Robert Schoenbaum. **p. 19:** Reprinted from The Amazing True Story of a Teenage Single
Mom by Katherine Arnoldi. Copyright ©1998 by Katherine Arnoldi. Published by Hyperion.
p. 33: Digital Imagery® copyright 1999 PhotoDisc, Inc. **p. 33:** Digital Imagery® copyright 1999
PhotoDisc, Inc. **p. 38:** © Kathryn Lemieux/Matt Tolbert. **p. 45:** © 2000 Star Tribune/Minneapolis–
St. Paul. **p. 51:** Associated Press/AP. **p. 58:** © Pat Wadecki. **p. 69:** *Newsweek,* © STONE/Bruce
Ayres, © STONE/Daniel Bosler, © Doug Martin/Photo Researchers, Inc., 1999 Newsweek, Inc. All
rights reserved. Reprinted with permission. **p. 72:** © TSM–Tom Stewart. **p. 81:** © Tom Bloom.
p. 88: © Adam Weiss. **p. 89:** © James D.Wilson. **p. 115:** © Hal Mayforth. **p. 125:** © William
Thomas Cain. **p. 136:** © Sara Krulwich/New York Times Pictures. **p. 144:** © Hulton Getty/Liaison
Agency. **p. 148:** Courtesy of the Freer Gallery of Art. **p. 161:** © David Turnley/CORBIS.

http://college.hmco.com

Printed in the U.S.A.

Library of Congress Catalog Card Number   00-104441

ISBN   0-395-97691-X

2 3 4 5 6 7 8 9-FFG-04 03 02 01

To our husbands,
John P. Keker and Laurence Best,
whose interest, assistance, and encouragement
enabled us to complete our two-book project

CONTENTS

INTRODUCTION

Journeys Near and Far: Reading and Responding Critically is a two-book interactive reading series with a writing component. Book 1 is directed to students at the intermediate level, and Book 2 to students at the high-intermediate level. The series is designed for students learning English in academic programs at the postsecondary level. A strong theoretical base and a cognitive orientation support the content, varied activities, and attention to critical thinking in the series.

Thought-provoking reading selections, diverse in their perspectives, are arranged thematically, appealing to students' sense of the familiar at first and then guiding them to explore the distant and less familiar. Book 1 opens with Chapter 1, "People in Our Lives," readings about Sammy Sosa, his family and his country; a young, heroic, single mother and her daughter; and the unforgettable experience of Odalis Tejada and his family, written while he was a college student. Chapter 2 explores ways of "Meeting That Special Someone," beginning with an essay on different ways of meeting people in the United States, continuing with two articles about a young man who found love "democratic style," and ending with a true essay by a young woman who met her future husband through a smile. Chapter 3, "Going Forward: Education and Employment," explores "How Open Am I to the Challenge of the University [or College]?" and continues with an article that examines behavior during the job interview. The chapter ends with a piece about a student, a worker-in-waiting, and two people in the work force and how they are working today. Chapter 4, "Looking Forward: Being a Wise Consumer in the United States," begins with advice from Consumers Union on how to be a smart consumer. The next selection focuses on the psychological aspect of pursuing affluence; the chapter ends with advice on how to be a wise user of the Internet. In the final chapter, "Looking Back," three people, Melissa Hacker, Duncan Hsu, and Nelson Mandela, look back at their lives while moving forward in them.

Chapters are linked by their common format, yet they remain independent of one another. Multiple sequences for presenting them are possible; the order of presentation can vary to account for factors affecting the classroom experience: guests on campus, an orientation or campus event theme, students' interests, or material covered in a concurrent course, for example. All supporting sections emphasize the active role of the students in the learning process. The activities in these sections engage students in the thoughtful reading and reflection that stimulate interest, promote inquiry, facilitate comprehension, aid developing vocabulary and reading strategies, generate critical oral and written response, and inspire confidence. The chapters in the book contain the following sections:

- **Opening Thought**
  A quotation or prompt and follow-up questions that guide students to discover the chapter's purpose

- **Discover What You Know, Think, Feel**
  A series of questions or activities that guide students to explore their knowledge about a selection's topic

- **Quick Comprehension Check**
  A summary of the selection's content done after the initial reading, which is a fill-in-the-blank activity using an answer bank for the first seven selections in the text; thereafter students generate their own answers for the blanks. This activity serves as presummary writing practice.

- **Questions for Thought and Discussion**
  A series of questions probing the selection's meaning, purpose, and relevance

- **Another Look at the Selection**
  Activities for examining closely a specific portion of the selection or applying information given in it

- **Vocabulary Building including Vocabulary Strategies and Exercises**
  Throughout the text specific vocabulary strategies are highlighted. Exercises help students apply these strategies while strengthening their vocabularies.

- **In Your Words**
  Prompts that help students express their own thoughts about the selections

- **Summing Up**
  A series of questions summarizing the work of the class, and discussion about a selection's topics

- **Reflecting and Synthesizing**
  A section concluding each chapter that enables students to integrate the material from the chapter into their own lives and experiences

Many of the activities in the different sections are suitable for pair, group, class, or independent work. The activities include prereading activities, previewing guides, reading comprehension questions, presummary and summary activities, oral activities, critical-thinking exercises, vocabulary strategies and vocabulary-building exercises, vocabulary log and double-entry reading journal, and questions and prompts that elicit written responses.

A specific feature in Book 1 is the highlighted vocabulary strategies: reading for meaning; using context; identifying key words; keeping a vocabulary log; using prefixes and suffixes accompanied by prefix and suffix charts and exercises; determining the job of a word in the sentence. Chapter 5 presents a summary of all of the strategies with exercises in which they are used. In addition, Book 1 includes practice with the alphabet as all glossaries and answer banks are in alphabetical order.

Every selection in each chapter is an authentic piece. Guided by Freire's pedagogy and Vygotsky's theories, we have not reduced the vocabulary in any of these selections. We have retained their rich sense, provided glossaries as well as vocabulary exercises for each selection, and stressed the importance of reading to understand the sense of a selection.

To the Student

The many students we have worked with inspired us to write *Journeys Near and Far: Reading and Responding Critically.* Our students wanted fresh and challenging material. They helped us understand what you might be interested in reading as you work to develop your English language skills. We hope you enjoy the reading selections, are inspired to respond to them, expand your vocabulary by developing vocabulary strategies, reading, and responding, and feel confident about what you have to say.

Jessie M. Reppy and Linda Best

ACKNOWLEDGMENTS

We extend our special thanks to the faculty, staff, and students of the English as a Second Language Program at Kean University, who are all part of the academic context that supported the design and development of the two-book series *Journeys Near and Far: Reading and Responding Critically.* We are especially grateful to the English as a Second Language students at Kean University who represent 55 countries. They have not only provided us with insight and input for preparing our materials but have generated our motivation and inspiration as well.

In addition, we would like to thank Susan Maguire, Director, World Languages: Marketing and ESL Publishing, for supporting our vision of the project and Kathy Sands Boehmer, Senior Associate Editor, for her editorial assistance. We also thank Manuel Muñoz, Editorial Assistant, for help with the process of preparing and submitting our manuscript. Moreover, we gratefully acknowledge the thoughtful critiques and suggestions from the following reviewers: Victoria Badalamenti, LaGuardia Community College; John Bagnole, OPIE/Ohio University; Ron Clark, CELO/Boston University; Janet Eveler, El Paso Community College; Frank Hermann, Houston Community College; Kathy Judd, Truman College; and Beth Pullman, DeKalb Technical Institute.

We also thank Dr. Betsy Rodriguez-Bachiller of Kean University for her professional and technical assistance as well as Barbara and Michael Best for their thought-provoking ideas and technical support.

JOURNEYS
NEAR
AND FAR 1

1

PEOPLE IN
OUR LIVES

OPENING THOUGHT

No man is an island entire of itself;
every man is a piece of the continent,
a part of the main...

John Donne (1572–1631), England

Take a few minutes to think about the words that introduce this chapter. Answer the following questions:

1. What do you think this quotation means?

_____

_____

_____

_____

2. Do you agree or disagree with it? Why?

_____

_____

_____

_____

3. Can you think of any examples to support your position?

_____

_____

_____

_____

Share your thoughts with your partner, group, or class.

Selection 1

DISCOVER WHAT YOU KNOW

What do you know about Sammy Sosa? Write down some things that you know about him. If you don't know anything, write, "I don't know anything." If there are things that you would like to know, write those, too.

_____

_____

_____

_____

PREVIEWING

Preview means to look at an entire selection quickly. Your purpose is to get an overview of the reading.

A. Answer the following questions as you preview this selection.

1. (a) What is the title?

_____

(b) What information do you know from this title?

_____

(c) What information do you need to know?

_____

2. (a) Who is the author?

_____

(b) What do you know about this author?

_____

3. (a) Where did this selection appear?

_____

(b) What do you know about this source?

_____

4. (a) Are there any pictures? _____ What does each picture show?

_____

(b) What information does the caption (the words under the picture) give?

_____

5. (a) Are there any words or sentences (do not include vocabulary from the Baseball Glossary) in a different kind of print? _____ Do you understand them? _____

(b) If no, which ones don't you understand? _____

_____

_____

6. (a) Now read quickly the first and last paragraphs of the article. What is the first paragraph about? _____

_____

_____

(b) What is the last paragraph about? _____

_____

7. Now read the rest of the paragraphs very quickly. From this quick reading write down what you think about the article. For example, is it interesting to you or not? Is it easy for you to read or not?

_____

_____

_____

8. What questions of your own did you have as you previewed the selection?

_____

_____

_____

_____

_____

_____

Now you have a general idea about the article and know what you can expect before you read it more carefully and completely. It is helpful to preview almost everything that you read, from recipes to textbooks. The process helps you to see the selection as a whole and the reading job ahead of you.

B. Next preview this map.

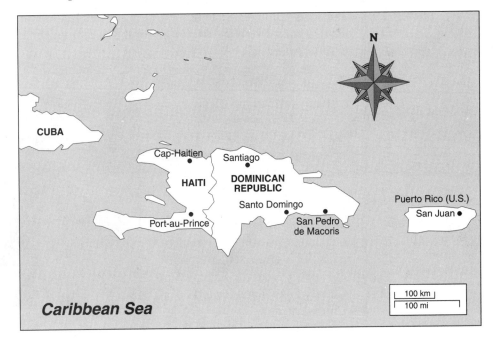

A MOST VALUABLE PLAYER (AND PROVIDER)

The skinny 16-year-old **lad,** who lived in a one-room apartment in San Pedro de Macoris, a small town in the Dominican Republic, with his **widowed** mother and four brothers and two sisters who were so poor that they ate just one meal a day, was in the airport in San Domingo and about to board a plane for America.

His mother was in tears. "Don't go," the boy's mother said.

"I've got to go," he said.

"If you go, we'll all die here," she said. The **lad,** after all, had shined shoes and washed cars to help earn enough money to put the rice and beans on the table for the family's meals.

"I've got to go, Mama," he said, "but I'll be back. And I will help us all."

And so in the summer of 1986, with a **bonus** of $3,500 to play baseball in the Texas Rangers organization, he flew off **to seek his fortune.**

And true to his promise, Sammy Sosa did come back. Most dramatically, perhaps was last October, after he, along with **Mark McGwire**, had hit so many **home runs** during the baseball season, 136 between them, that they became two of the most famous people in not just America, but also many parts of the world. He was, among other notable moments, invited to attend President Clinton's State of the Union address last month, and Pope John Paul II praised him and McGwire for their accomplishments in his recent visit to America.

When Sosa returned to the Dominican Republic in October, it was a short time after Hurricane Georges had virtually **leveled** the island. Thousands were homeless, more than 200 had been killed. He had personally sought and received a donation from Major League Baseball to help in relief— baseball gave $1 million. Sosa also had given a large sum of his own money as well as directing parts of his **endorsement** money and money from the Sammy Sosa Charity Foundation toward Dominican aid.

"When I got off the plane at Las Americas airport," Sosa said

Sammy Sosa received the most valuable player award in Manhattan.

40 yesterday in a Manhattan hotel, "there was something like a half-million people there to greet me. It was one of the most **thrilling** moments of my life. The President of my country, Leonel Fernandez, had declared a national holiday on the day of my return. Then the people cheered when I drove through the streets, where the wood from the torn-down houses was still scattered all around. For just a moment, anyway, everybody forgot about the hurricane."

45 Sosa was in town yesterday to receive his National League most valuable player award for 1998 at the annual dinner of the New York chapter of the Baseball Writers Association. He had one of the greatest years in baseball history, hitting 66 **homers**—just four short of McGwire's record—batting in 158 **runs,** scoring 134 **runs** and **hitting .308,** and playing **right field** for the

50 **playoff-bound** Chicago Cubs about as well as he produced at the **plate.** In his spare time, the **slugger stole 18 bases.**

It turned out that Sosa's mother, Lucrecia, had little to worry about when her fifth of seven children departed for the United States. He recently bought a comfortable house for her, and when she gets restless she may sleep in one

55 of the eight bedrooms in the house Sosa is building for himself in Santo Domingo. He has been able to do this on a four-year contract he signed two years ago with the Cubs for $42.5 million. And the **endorsements** and other business opportunities he **has capitalized on** recently will earn him an **estimated** $10 million more per year.

60 Sosa left school in the seventh grade because his mother, after his father's death, needed him to help support the family. It's a well-known story now how Sosa would shine the shoes and wash the cars of baseball stars from the Dominican Republic like George Bell and Pedro Guerrero and Joaquin Andujar. He dreamed of having what they had. And he has seen some of

65 them **fall on hard times.**

"This is a mirror for me," he said. "I am careful with what I have. When you've been as poor as I have, you never forget it. You know you can lose what you have. I try not to be foolish."

. . . As to next season, will he feel pressure to equal or **surpass** last season?

70 "Baseball is not pressure," he said. "Pressure is when you're 7 years old and you don't have food to eat. I used to cry a lot, inside. So when you've come from nowhere and have all that I have now, I sleep like a baby every night.

"And even after all that's gone on this **off season,** I feel mentally and physically ready to play this season. Even if I hit 10 **homers** next season—

75 yes, 10 **homers!**—it will be a success because I'll be trying my best. But I am **confident.** So I say, 'Let the show begin.'"

Ira Berkow

BASEBALL GLOSSARY

Below is a list of baseball or "specialized" vocabulary for this reading. If you are unfamiliar with baseball, this list will help you understand a little about the sport and so will help you to understand the reading selection better.

base (n.) any one of the four corners of an infield, marked by a bag or plate

hit .308 (v.) to have a batting average of .308—a very good average

home plate (n.) a rubber marker beside which the batter stands; home base

home run (n.) a hit that allows the batter to touch all four bases and score a run or a point for the team

homer (n.) home run

Mark McGwire (name) a baseball player for the St. Louis Cardinals who hit 70 home runs in the 1998 baseball season. He set a new record for home runs.

off season (n.) the time of year when a sport is not played

playoff (n.) a game or series of games played to determine a championship or break a tie

right field (n.) the right side of the outfield; **right fielder** (n.) the baseball player who covers it. Sammy Sosa plays this position.

run (n.) a score in baseball made by a player reaching home plate safely

slugger (n.) a player who hits the baseball hard and deep

steal bases (v.) to run to other bases when no player on the opposite team is able to touch you

QUICK COMPREHENSION CHECK

Complete the sentences with words or phrases from the answer bank below.

a lot of   didn't want
baseball   had to
because she was afraid   helped many people
bought a house   successful
confident   the Dominican Republic

Sammy Sosa is a **(1)** _____ player from **(2)** _____. His mother **(3)** _____ him to come to the United States **(4)** _____. But he told her that he **(5)** _____ leave. He had a very **(6)** _____ career and earned **(7)** _____ money. When he returned to his country, he **(8)** _____. He also **(9)** _____ for his mother. At the end of the reading selection, Sammy is **(10)** _____ about his next season.

Read the selection a second time. If necessary, change answers above. Then answer the following questions.

QUESTIONS FOR THOUGHT AND DISCUSSION

1. Why is Sammy Sosa called "A Most Valuable Player" in the title of the article?

2. Why is "(and Provider)" added to the title?

3. What kind of background did Sammy Sosa come from?

4. Why did Sammy's mother say, "If you go, we'll all die here"?

5. Why did Sammy say, "I've got to go, Mama"?

6. What happened in Sammy's country while he was in the United States?

7. List three things that Sammy did for his country and/or family.

8. What kind of life is Sammy living now?

9. Is hitting 10 home runs good in baseball? Why does Sammy say that if he hits 10 home runs in the next season, it will be a success?

10. How do you think that Sammy will live his life in the future? List the lines in the selection that support your thinking.

11. What can you say about Sammy and the quotation at the beginning of this chapter?

ANOTHER LOOK AT THE SELECTION

Read the selection again and do the following exercises.
You can do the exercises in pairs or groups.

1. In what tense or time is this article mainly written? _____

Why? _____

2. List the events in Sosa's life that are described at the following times. Also note the lines in the selection where these events are discussed.

    A. summer 1986 _____

    B. October 1998 _____

    C. 1998 Chicago Cubs Baseball Season _____

    D. yesterday _____

    E. two years ago _____

What can you say about the sequence or order of the times described? Do they follow a chronological order (a strict order by time)? _____

Why do you think the author, Ira Berkow, chose this way of presenting the events in Sosa's life? _____

_____

3. In the following paragraph from the selection, circle all of the simple past-tense verbs. If there are any time markers, such as *yesterday,* or *last week,* in the paragraph, underline them. A sample sentence is done for you.

> Sosa (left) school <u>in the seventh grade</u> because his mother, <u>after his father's death,</u> (needed) him to help support the family.

> And true to his promise, Sammy Sosa did come back. Most dramatically, perhaps, was last October. He and Mark McGwire hit so many home runs during the 1998 baseball season, 136 between them, that they became two of the most famous people in not just America, but also many parts of the world. President Clinton invited Sosa to attend his State of the Union address last month, and Pope John Paul II praised him and McGwire for their accomplishments in his recent visit to America.

4. Now do the same in this paragraph:

> "When I got off the plane at Las Americas airport," Sosa said yesterday in a Manhattan hotel, "there was something like a half-million people there to greet me. It was one of the most thrilling moments of my life. The President of my country, Leonel Fernandez, had declared a national holiday on the day of my

return. Then the people cheered when I drove through the streets, where the wood from the torn-down houses was still scattered all around. For just a moment, anyway, everybody forgot about the hurricane."

5. Look at the last two paragraphs of the selection. Which two tenses are used most in in these paragraphs?

_____

_____

VOCABULARY BUILDING

> **VOCABULARY STRATEGY:**
> Vocabulary study is very important, but as you read, keep in mind that you are reading for the **meaning** of the selection. Do not get lost in the study of each word. The vocabulary exercises in each chapter will help you to build your vocabulary so that reading for meaning will become easier as you go. If you need to know the meaning of the word, the first thing to do is to try to get it from context (the words and sentences around the word). If you cannot, look it up in the dictionary.

Exercise 1: Find the following words in the selection. They are in bold print to help you find them quickly. Use the context (the words and sentences around the word) to help you get the meaning. Write it in the blank. If you cannot get the meaning from the context, check the dictionary. Two examples are done for you.

Example 1: lad (n.)   a young man (Context: 16 years old)

Example 2: surpass (v.)   "surpass" last season: not "equal," but the context doesn't really help. (Dictionary definition: to go beyond in degree or quality.) "To go beyond" last season

1. widowed (adj.) _____

2. bonus (n.) _____

3. level (v.) _____

4. endorsement (n., adj.) endorsements (n.) _____

5. capitalize on (v.) _____

6. estimated (adj.) _____

7. confident (adj.) _____

Answer these questions in writing: Did the context help you with any vocabulary? Which ones? Did you have to look up any words in the dictionary? If "Yes," which ones?

_____

_____

Exercise 2: Complete the sentences with one of the expressions from the list. If you don't know the word, go back to the selection and find it. The expressions are in bold print. Then try to get the meaning from context. If you cannot, check it in the dictionary. You may have to change the form of some words to complete the sentences.

Nouns	Verbs and Verb Phrases	Adjectives
bonus	to capitalize on	confident
endorsement (also adj.)	to fall on hard times	estimated
lad	to level	thrilling
	to seek his fortune	widowed
	to surpass	

1. When Sammy Sosa was a young _____ in the seventh grade, his father died.

2. His mother, Lucretia Sosa, was _____, with seven children to support.

3. Against his mother's wishes, Sammy left the Dominican Republic _____ in the United States.

4. Sammy received a _____ when he signed to play baseball in the Texas Rangers organization.

5. Sammy made a lot of money through _____.

6. After a hurricane _____ the Dominican Republic, Sosa gave a lot of aid to his country.

7. It was _____ for baseball fans to watch as McGwire and Sosa hit so many home runs.

8. Sammy is determined that he will not _____ as he has seen some other baseball stars do.

9. He _____ his fame by making very good business deals.

10. The business deals will earn him an _____
    $10 million outside of his $42.5 million four-year baseball contract.

11. Everyone is wondering whether Sammy is going to _____
    the number of home runs that he hit last season.

12. At the end of the reading, Sammy seems very satisfied and _____.

IN YOUR WORDS

Write a few sentences to answer the following questions.

1. What fact did you learn from the selection that you did not know?

   _____

   _____

2. How is Sammy Sosa presented in this selection?

   _____

   _____

3. What is your opinion of Sammy Sosa?

   _____

   _____

SUMMING UP

Share your answers to these questions with your partner, group, or class:

1. What facts did you learn from the selection that you did not know? Did any members choose the same fact?

2. Did you all agree on how Sammy Sosa is presented in the selection? If not, where is the disagreement? Be prepared to support what you say with lines from the selection.

3. Do you all share the same opinion of Sammy Sosa? Why or why not?

4. After all the groups have presented their views, answer the following:

What does the class think of Sammy Sosa?

DISCOVER WHAT YOU THINK

Free association is the reporting of the first thought that comes to mind in response to a given stimulus (for example, a word). You will be using free association when you do the following:

Write down what comes into your mind when you hear

1. Superman _____

2. mother _____

3. "A Mother: Young, Single and Heroic" _____

_____

Share your thoughts with your partner, group, or class.

PREVIEWING

Using what you have learned about previewing from the first selection, preview the reading selection.

1. (a) What is the title?

_____

(b) What information do you know from this title?

_____

(c) What information do you need to know?

_____

2. (a) Who is the author?

_____

(b) What do you know about this author?

_____

3. (a) Where did this selection appear?

_____

(b) What do you know about this source?

_____

4. (a) Are there any pictures? _____

(b) What does each picture show?

_____

(c) What information is given in the caption of each picture?

_____

5. a) Are there any words or sentences (do not include vocabulary from the Glossary) in a different kind of print? _____ Do you understand them? _____

(b) If no, which ones don't you understand? _____

_____

_____

6. Now read quickly the first and last paragraphs of the selection.

(a) What is the first paragraph about? _____

_____

(b) What is the last paragraph about? _____

_____

7. Now read the rest of the paragraphs very quickly. From this quick reading, write down what you think about the article.

_____

_____

8. What questions of your own did you have as you previewed the selection?

_____

_____

A MOTHER: YOUNG, SINGLE AND HEROIC

Who says a superhero needs **rippling** muscles to beat back the forces of evil? Does the crusader really need a cape **to soar** through the heavens and come to the rescue? For that matter, who says he has to be a he?

Katherine Arnoldi has spent years drawing the crash-bang adventures of a skinny heroine whose only costume is a black skirt and striped top. Her **superheroine** has a **sidekick**—her infant daughter. She also has plenty of **close calls** with death—working among toxic chemicals in a factory or being beaten by an abusive boyfriend. Her story is about the daily down-to-earth hassles and heroics of a teen-age single mom. But as in any good comic book, her heroine finally gets her chance to fly. So what if she **doesn't duck into** a phone booth for a quick change? All she needed was her college acceptance letter and she floated off the page.

"The Amazing 'True' Story of a Teenage Single Mom" (Hyperion) is mostly her own tale of becoming a single mother when she was 17 in the early 1970s. The **graphic** novel **recounts** the shame others heaped on her, the dreary jobs she took to support her daughter, and her brushes with bad bosses and boyfriends. At its core is the story of her own unyielding—though at times barely sustained—hope and courage that allowed her to come into her own in college. It is a message she now spreads in occasional visits to programs for teen-age mothers around the city where she shares her story and book with young women who had to put aside their childhood dreams.

"I thought only rich people went to college," she said. "Sometimes I say my book is a **support group** you can hold in your hand. I'm just grateful it's in a lot of hands that are maybe **isolated.**"

Ms. Arnoldi, 46, started her book in the mid-1980's, when she was living on the Lower East Side (section of New York City) with her daughter, Stacie, after she graduated from the University of Arkansas and began working at different jobs. Her own faith in education had already prompted her to start visiting **high-school equivalency programs** with stacks of college application forms and college guides.

Katherine Arnoldi, superhero

40 "A lot of times I would give them the forms and the women would tell me, 'Yeah, but I have to go now,'" she recalled. "They would get up and leave. So I felt maybe if I told them my story it would be different."

She started handing out copies of scenes and pages from her book, which was then a work in progress. In her drawings, as in her life, there were times when faith and hope looked like tiny compartments in her brain, almost
45 squeezed into insignificance by more **mundane** or **pressing** concerns.

"There was more room in my brain for the names of the people in the **'Beverly Hillbillies,'**" she joked. "Why did hope live? I didn't feel worthy. But I knew my daughter was worthy. I brought that up and held it in front of me."

She raised her hand to her face.
50 "I moved forward, like this," she said. "Here's my child. I know my child is worthy. I think I trusted that."

She **persevered** to see Stacie graduate from college and become a research assistant who is applying to medical school.

But she had less success at first with publishers, who passed on the book,
55 thinking there was no market for it. "Oh, the country's 25 million single mothers are not a market," she said. "To me, that's just stupidity. If single mothers decided **to boycott Pampers,** people would take notice."

People are noticing Ms. Arnoldi now. She figures somebody has to speak on behalf of mothers who have been **vilified** in the national debate over
60 **social policy.** If policy makers want to talk about individual responsibility, she said, what about the responsibility of colleges and the government to offer **adequate** day care and housing for single mothers?

"Single mothers have been **portrayed** as **welfare queens** without any personal responsibility," she said. "Like, it wasn't the **savings and loans** that
65 caused the **recession.** It was single moms."

A baby was making goo-goo sounds recently as Ms. Arnoldi shared her story with a group of single mothers studying for their **high-school equivalency diplomas** at a Bronx (borough of New York City) community center. The young women told her they wanted to study computers, child
70 care, business.

Ms. Arnoldi handed out copies of her book. Then she helped the young women fill out postcards that they would send to colleges asking for application forms. Behind her was a poster. It read, "Anyone Can Be a Leader."

"For 20 cents you can change your life," she said as she handed out the
75 postcards. "It changed mine."

She sounded just super.

David Gonzalez

GLOSSARY

Beverly Hillbillies (name) a comedy on television in the l960s about some country people from the mountains (hillbillies) who went to live in Beverly Hills, California

crusader (n.) one who campaigns for a belief or ideal, for example, against evil

duck [into] (v.) to enter quickly

high-school equivalency program (n.) a program for people who have left high school before they graduated. They study and take tests to receive a **high-school equivalency diploma.**

Pampers (name) the name of a kind of diapers for babies

portrayed (v.) pictured, described

recession (n.) a time when economic activity is weak

rippling (adj.) showing small waves on the surface

savings and loans [institution(s)] (n.) a kind of bank that takes savings deposits and makes mortgage loans. In the 1980s savings and loans were allowed to take checking accounts and make business loans with very bad economic results. This caused a **recession.**

social policy (n.) a government plan for a society (the people of a country)

support group (n.) people with a common concern, such as single mothers, who meet in a group to give encouragement to one another

vilified (v.) spoken about in an extremely negative way

welfare queen (n.) an uncomplimentary expression describing a woman who cheats by drawing more than one welfare check

QUICK COMPREHENSION CHECK

Complete the sentences with a word or phrase from the answer bank below. Preview the Quick Comprehension Check to get an idea of the sentences.

book	helps other single teen-age moms	single mother
college	her experiences	Stacie
daughter	Katherine Arnoldi	very difficult

An illustration by Katherine Arnoldi from her book showing her and her sidekick, Stacie

This article is about **(1)** _____ who

became a **(2)** _____ at 17. She had a

(3) _____ named **(4)** _____.

Her life was **(5)** _____. But she went to

(6) _____ and graduated. In the 1980s she

started writing a **(7)** _____ about

(8) _____. Now she **(9)** _____.

Read the selection again. If necessary, change answers above.

SCANNING

Scan means to run your eyes quickly over a reading to find a specific piece of information. You most likely have been scanning to find answers to the questions asked above. Now practice scanning with more awareness as you answer the questions below.

QUESTIONS FOR THOUGHT AND DISCUSSION

1. What is the author's message in the first paragraph?

2. Who is the main character in the selection and what two major events changed her life?

3. When she started visiting high-school equivalency groups with college applications, was she successful? Why or why not? What did she do next?

4. Where did she find inspiration in her life?

5. What is her opinion about single mothers as a market?

6. What does she think about the position of single mothers in the United States?

7. What does she think that colleges and the government should do for single mothers?

8. Why does the author end the selection with, "She sounded just super."?

9. What kind of life do you think Katherine Arnoldi will have in the future? Are there any lines in the selection that support your view?

10. What can you say about Arnoldi and the quotation at the beginning of this chapter?

ANOTHER LOOK AT THE SELECTION

The following exercises can be done in pairs or groups:

1. Read the first paragraph of the selection, which is printed below. What do you notice about it? Why do you think that David Gonzalez wrote it this way?

   Who says a superhero needs rippling muscles to beat back the forces of evil? Does the crusader really need a cape to soar through the heavens and come to the rescue? For that matter, who says he has to be a he?

2. What sentences in the selection build on the image or picture of Katherine Arnoldi introduced in the first paragraph? Give the numbers of the lines for the sentences.

3. In the following paragraph from the selection, circle all of the simple past-tense verbs. If there are any time markers, such as *yesterday,* or *last week,* in the paragraph, underline them.

   Ms. Arnoldi, 46, started her book in the mid-1980's, when she was living on the Lower East Side (section of New York City) with her daughter, Stacie, after she graduated from the University of Arkansas and began working at different jobs. Her own faith in education had already prompted her to start visiting high-school equivalency programs with stacks of college application forms and college guides.

4. Do the same for the following paragraphs.

"There was more room in my brain for the names of the people in the 'Beverly Hillbillies,'" she joked. "Why did hope live? I didn't feel worthy. But I knew my daughter was worthy. I brought that up and held it in front of me."

She raised her hand to her face.

"I moved forward, like this," she said. Here's my child. I know my child is worthy. I think I trusted that."

She persevered to see Stacie graduate from college and become a research assistant who is applying to medical school.

VOCABULARY BUILDING

> **VOCABULARY STRATEGY:**
> A **key word** is a word that you must know in order to understand the meaning of the reading. It may be repeated more than once in the selection. First, try to get the meaning of the key word from context. If you cannot, look it up in the dictionary.

Exercise 1: In the following paragraph from the reading, which word is a key word? _____

What does it mean? _____

Is *Beverly Hillbillies* a key word? _____ Why or why not?

_____

"There was more room in my brain for the names of the people in the 'Beverly Hillbillies,'" she joked. "Why did hope live? I didn't feel worthy. But I knew my daughter was worthy. I brought that up and held it in front of me."

She raised her hand to her face.

"I moved forward, like this," she said. "Here's my child. I know my child is worthy. I think I trusted that."

When you are reading, do you have to look up in the dictionary every word that you do not know? Why or why not? _____

Exercise 2: Read the second paragraph of the selection. What is a key word in this paragraph? What does it mean? _____

Exercise 3: Match the following words or expressions from Selection 2 with their meanings. First scan the selection to find the words and expressions. They are in bold print to help you find them easily. Examine the context and decide if you can understand the meaning from it. If you cannot, check the dictionary. Write the letter of your choice in the space.

Vocabulary

_____ **1.** adequate (adj.)

_____ **2.** boycott (v.)

_____ **3.** close call (n.)

_____ **4.** graphic (adj.)

_____ **5.** isolated (adj.)

_____ **6.** mundane (adj.)

_____ **7.** persevere (v.)

_____ **8.** pressing (adj.)

_____ **9.** recount (v.)

_____ **10.** sidekick (n.)

_____ **11.** soar (v.)

_____ **12.** superheroine (n.)

Meanings

a. needing immediate attention

b. to fly

c. a situation in which something dangerous or unwanted almost happens

d. to tell something in detail

e. alone or cut off from people

f. to hold to a purpose in spite of opposition or discouragement

g. to act together in refusing to buy something, especially as an expression of protest

h. described in clear and vivid detail

i. a close friend or companion

j. not interesting; ordinary

k. a superior woman, famous for courageous acts or significant achievements

l. enough

Exercise 4: Complete the sentences with the correct vocabulary from Exercise 3. You may have to change the form of some of the words.

1. Some famous heroes _____ in the sky.

2. In her book "The Amazing 'True' Story of a Teenage Single Mom" the

   skinny _____ wears a striped top and a black skirt.

3. Her _____ in the book is her infant daughter.

4. In the book Arnoldi _____ many events from her own life.

5. In the life of a single mother there are many _____ everyday jobs.

6. As well, there are many _____ problems, such as how to support oneself and the child.

7. Arnoldi presents a _____ description of her problems in her novel.

8. In fact, while working in a toxic chemical factory, the character in the novel has a _____ with death.

9. She _____ to see her daughter become a professional.

10. Arnoldi believes that single mothers may feel _____ and that her book could help them.

11. If 25 million single mothers _____ a particular product, people in business would notice.

12. Arnoldi thinks that colleges and the government should provide _____ facilities for single mothers.

VOCABULARY STRATEGY:
Another way to build your vocabulary is to keep your own **vocabulary log** or **journal**. Choose words that you want to teach yourself. Write down the word, the sentence where it is used, and the meaning. You can also note how the word is used: noun, pronoun, verb, adjective, adverb, preposition, conjunction.

Example: **brush** (n.)   Sentence: The graphic novel recounts the shame others heaped on her, and the dreary jobs she took to support her daughter, and her <u>brushes</u> with bad bosses and boyfriends.

Meaning: a brief, often hostile or frightening meeting

Choose at least five words from Selection 1 and five words from Selection 2. Enter them in your vocabulary log.

IN YOUR WORDS

Write a few sentences to answer the following questions.

1. Which part of the selection is your favorite?

_____

_____

2. How is Katherine Arnoldi presented in the selection?

_____

_____

3. What is your opinion of her?

_____

_____

4. What do you think about the ending of the selection? Reread the last two paragraphs before writing this answer.

_____

_____

SUMMING UP

Share your answers to the following.

1. Did you all choose the same favorite part? You may wish to read your favorite part to the group.

2. Did you all agree on how Katherine Arnoldi is presented in the selection? If not, where is the disagreement? Be prepared to support your position with lines from the selection.

3. Do you all share the same opinion of Katherine Arnoldi? Why or why not?

4. After the groups have presented their views, answer the following:

> ### What does the class think of Katherine Arnoldi?

Selection 3

DISCOVER YOURSELF

Have you ever felt like an island, alone with no one who cared for you? Freewrite about that time. When freewriting, do not worry about language (grammar, vocabulary, spelling). Just write what comes into your mind about the topic. Freewriting is only for you. It will not be evaluated by your teacher. Start writing and do not stop until your teacher tells you to.

PREVIEWING

The short questions below will help you remember the preview process. If you need to, refer to the complete set of preview questions for Selections 1 and 2.

1. Title? _____

2. Author? _____

3. Source? _____

4. Pictures? _____

 Captions? _____

5. Words or sentences in different print? _____

 _____

6. First paragraph? _____

 Last paragraph? _____

7. A quick read through the whole selection. Impression of the selection?

 _____

 _____

8. Your questions about the selection?

 _____

 _____

PEOPLE IN OUR LIVES

AN UNFORGETTABLE EXPERIENCE

Many people in this world have experienced an event that has had great **impact** on their lives. I am a human being and, like many other people, I have experienced more than one significant event from which I have learned very important things. Although the event that I am going to describe in the following essay was a negative experience, it was of great significance to me. From it I learned a very important lesson which has helped me to think a little more before I make some decisions.

In my first years of **adolescence** I had some friends whom I considered good friends, but I was wrong: they were bad. They were very important to me, and many times I was influenced by them to participate in negative and **illegal** activities. At the time I was living with my parents. They were very proud of me because I liked to study, go to church, and engage in other good activities. As time passed, I became more interested in my friends than in school or my family. Many times I would go to school but my friends, who didn't study, **persuaded** me to join them instead. I took many risks with them—and even got arrested. As a result, I **flunked** the school year and spoiled the good image that my family and other people had of me.

Soon my parents began to give me advice concerning my friends and the changes that I had to make in order to regain my good standing. They told me the results that I would get if I continued doing all the things that my friends did. But I didn't pay attention to my parents' advice because I thought that I was perfect and that I knew everything. So, I continued to be close to my friends. Every day I would return later and later to my home from places where I went with them. I got angry with my mother because she waited up for me every night in the living room. She wouldn't go to bed until I arrived at the house. It didn't matter what time it was.

Then my father warned me that he would send me to special prison designed for teenagers who **demonstrate** poor social behavior. When my father told me this, I didn't pay attention to him because I was sure that my father loved me too much to do that to me.

Odalis graduated from Kean University, Union, New Jersey, in 1998.

Time passed, and I didn't change. One Friday night I stayed at my house, something very unusual for me at that time. My parents were happy because they thought I wasn't going to go out with my friends that night. However, around 10:30 P.M., when I was ready to go to bed, three of my friends arrived at my house. They wanted to go to a party that night and wanted me to be with them. I agreed and put on my clothes. When my parents realized that I was going to the party, they told me that if I did, I couldn't come back to my house ever again. But I went anyway. When I left, I looked at my home and could hear my mother crying. I tried to return home, but my friends told me that I was a man and could do whatever I wanted.

A few minutes later we arrived at the party. There were many teenagers and adults, many of them drunk. I took a seat at a table with my friend. That night, there was a **raid.** The police had come to search the house. Upon **inspection,** the cops found a gun on one of my friends and on another they found marijuana. I was in shock because I didn't know about it. Although I was innocent, I was placed under arrest because I was with them. My friends and I were taken to different places by the police because they wanted to **interrogate** us. Two of my friends were found innocent and picked up by their **respective** parents. I was found innocent, but because I was a teenager, I couldn't get out of jail until my parents signed some papers.

When I **realized** that I was alone without anybody to help me to get out of jail, I cried. Then, I began to think about the advice that my parents had given me a few days and a few hours ago. I wanted to call home but couldn't because my parents had told me that if I left for the party with my friends I couldn't return ever again. So I called my friends, but they said they didn't know me. I felt how bad and painful it was to be alone, without parents, without friends—without anyone.

Finally, three days after my arrest, my parents took pity on me and came to take me out of jail. Those three days in prison seemed like three centuries. I experienced some feelings that are difficult to forget.

When I got home, I was very happy because I had thought that I would never see my family again. I was **grateful** that God had given me an opportunity to return. I got emotional because I had my family as I did before when everything was beautiful and peaceful. I could feel the love that my family had for me and my importance to them. Now I could understand why my parents had given me all their advice. I **realized** that my parents had only wanted me to succeed and that my friends just wanted my downfall.

Odalis Tejada
Santiago, Dominican Republic

QUICK COMPREHENSION CHECK ✅

Complete the sentences with a word or phrase from the answer bank below. Remember to preview the sentences.

family	party
friends	police raid
get him out	realized that his family loved him very much
gun	school
his parents	the Dominican Republic
in jail	teenager
marijuana	that he couldn't return home
Odalis Tejada	three days

The essay was written by **(1)** _____ who is from **(2)** _____. He lived with his **(3)** _____. He became more interested in his **(4)** _____ than his **(5)** _____ and **(6)** _____. One Friday night his friends wanted him to go to a **(7)** _____. His parents told him **(8)** _____ if he went, but he went anyway. That night there was a **(9)** _____ during which a **(10)** _____ and **(11)** _____ were found. He ended up **(12)** _____. Since he was a **(13)** _____, his parents had to **(14)** _____. He spent **(15)** _____ there before his parents came. After this experience, he **(16)** _____.

Read the selection again. Then answer the questions on the next page using scanning to help you find the answers.

QUESTIONS FOR THOUGHT AND DISCUSSION

1. Describe Odalis's friends.
2. What advice did Odalis's parents give to him?
3. How did Odalis react to this advice?
4. What did Odalis's father finally say and how did Odalis react to this?
5. What did Odalis's parents say would happen to him if he went to the late-night party against their wishes?
6. How did Odalis's friends pressure him to go with them?
7. What happened at the party?
8. What happened to Odalis?
9. How did Odalis's friends answer when he asked them to help him?
10. Why didn't Odalis call his parents?
11. How long did Odalis spend in jail?
12. Explain how Odalis felt about his parents' advice after his experience.

ANOTHER LOOK AT THE SELECTION

The following can be done in pairs or groups:

1. List the events that happened to Odalis on Friday night. Are they listed in the selection in a strict chronological order or not? Which kind of order do you think is easier to write, strict chronological order or an order in which you move back and forth between present and past? Why?

2. Make three lists. In short sentences describe the behavior of Odalis (a) before he met his friends, (b) while he knew them, and (c) after his experience in jail.

   (a) ―――――――――――――――――――――――――――――

   (b) ―――――――――――――――――――――――――――――

   (c) ―――――――――――――――――――――――――――――

3. Which tense does Odalis mainly use in his essay? Read the essay again paragraph by paragraph and note the main tense for each.

VOCABULARY BUILDING

REMINDER:
Add at least five new vocabulary words from Selection 3 to your vocabulary log.

Exercise 1: Match the following words or expressions from Selection 3 with their meanings. First, scan the selection to find them. They are in bold print to help you find them easily. Examine the context and decide if you can understand the meaning from it. If you cannot, check the dictionary.

Vocabulary

_____ **1.** adolescence (n.)

_____ **2.** demonstrate (v.)

_____ **3.** flunk (v.)

_____ **4.** grateful (adj.)

_____ **5.** illegal (adj.)

_____ **6.** impact (n.)

_____ **7.** inspection (n.)

_____ **8.** interrogate (v.)

_____ **9.** persuade (v.)

_____ **10.** raid (n.)

_____ **11.** realize (v.)

_____ **12.** respective (adj.)

Meanings

a. effect of something

b. to comprehend completely or correctly

c. to question somebody formally and closely

d. a sudden forcible entry into a place by police

e. the period of growth and physical development that leads from childhood to adulthood

f. to show clearly and deliberately

g. to convince

h. to fail

i. official examination

j. appreciative or thankful for some good received

k. against the law

l. relating to two or more persons regarded individually

Exercise 2: Complete the sentences with the correct vocabulary from Exercise 1. One word is not used at all. You may have to change the form of some words to fit in the blanks.

1. Odalis had a very difficult _____.

2. He had some friends who _____ him to get involved in _____ activities.

3. He even _____ the school year because he didn't study.

4. Odalis had one particular experience that had a great _____ on him.

5. One Friday night he went to a party with his friends where a police _____ took place.

6. The police did an _____ and found a gun and marijuana.

7. Though innocent, Odalis was taken to jail where the police _____ him.

8. After his experience in jail, Odalis _____ that his parents loved him very much.

9. He also saw that they _____ their love for him by all the advice they had given him.

10. Finally, he was _____ to God for giving him the opportunity to be with his family again.

IN YOUR WORDS

Write a few sentences to answer the following questions.

1. Odalis spent three days in jail before his parents came to get him. Was this good for him or not? Why or why not?

   _____

   _____

2. What do you think of the decision of Odalis's parents to leave him there?

   _____

   _____

3. What questions would you like to ask Odalis?

   _____

   _____

4. Discuss Odalis and the quotation that opened this chapter.

   _____

   _____

   _____

SUMMING UP

Share your answers to the questions above with the class.

1. Did you all agree on the answers to the first two questions above?

2. Make a list of questions that the class would like to ask Odalis.

3. What observations does the class have about Odalis and the lines at the beginning of the chapter?

REFLECTING AND SYNTHESIZING

A. Share your vocabulary logs with a partner or group. Did you choose any of the same words? Add more words to your log as a result of the discussion if you wish.

B. After answering the following, share your thoughts with your partner, group, or class.

1. Based on information in the reading selections, were Sammy Sosa, Katherine Arnoldi, and Odalis Tejada continents or islands or both? Write a few sentences about each person that state your views.

2. Which selection did you like the best? Why?

3. For the person in the selection that you chose, write a few sentences about the effects he/she had on people or that people had on him/her.

4. Which selection did you find easiest to read? Which was the hardest? Why?

C. Answer these on your own.

1. Choose one of the people that you read about in this chapter: Sammy Sosa, Katherine Arnoldi, or Odalis Tejada. Write about what you learned from her or his life. How would you apply it to your life?

2. Make a list of people who had an influence on you or on whom you had an influence.

3. Select one person from your list and freewrite about that person. Read your freewriting and underline the parts that you like.

4. Describe an event that shows how the person influenced you or you influenced the person.

5. Write about yourself: Do you feel that you are an island or a continent? Have you ever felt like an island? Give examples from your life. Note: In this question, you must write about your feelings of being alone (an island) or connected (a continent).

6. Are there any quotations in your language that are similar to John Donne's? If so, write them down and explain them. Give examples to illustrate them.

2

MEETING THAT SPECIAL SOMEONE

OPENING THOUGHT

A Happy Love
A happy love. Is it normal,
is it serious, is it profitable—
what use to the world are two
people who have no eyes for the world?*

Wislawa Szymborska (1923–), Poland

Share your thoughts with your partner, group, or class.

The Nobel Prize** winning poet asks four questions about a happy love. How would you answer them?

1. Is a happy love normal?

_____

_____

2. Is it serious?

_____

_____

3. Is it profitable?

_____

_____

4. What use to the world are two people who have no eyes for the world?

_____

_____

Share your thoughts with your partner, group, or class.

---

*From *Sounds Feelings Thoughts: Seventy Poems by Wislawa Szymborska.* Copyright © 1981 by Princeton University Press. Reprinted by permission of Princeton University Press.

**Any of the six international prizes awarded each year by the Nobel Foundation for outstanding achievements in certain fields including literature. Alfred Bernhard Nobel (1833–96) of Sweden, who invented dynamite, gave his fortune to finance the Nobel Prizes.

Selection 1

DISCOVER WHAT YOU KNOW

1. List below the ways a person today can meet "a happy love."

_____

_____

_____

_____

_____

_____

2. Which do you think is the best way to meet that special person?

_____

_____

_____

_____

_____

_____

3. Why did you choose that way?

_____

_____

_____

_____

MEETING SOMEONE SPECIAL IN THE UNITED STATES

In the United States there are several ways that people can find "that special someone" without having to go on a **blind date** or **actually** meeting the person. Personal newspaper **advertisements,** dating services, and **Internet chat rooms** and **Web sites** can all **assist** a person to find a partner.

5   Placing a personal **advertisement** in the newspaper is one way to find a partner. To **submit** a personal **ad** in some newspapers a person must be at least 18 years of age. Placing the ad and a voice greeting to accompany it may be free. There may also be free message **retrieval** once a week. To respond to advertisements a person must dial a 900 number and give the

10 box number of the ad. The person may choose to leave a response or not. The charge for using the 900 number is usually about $2.00 per minute. A person can also **browse** through **ads** and listen to a number of voice introductions before making a choice. Some newspapers also state how many new advertisements there are each week. A reader can then scan to

15 find the new ads.

Some sample advertisements follow. Which person would you like to meet?

GREET AND MEET

Seeking Serious Relationship

Divorced, white female with two children, seeking mature, widowed or divorced male, with children, who likes movies, playing sports, and dinners at home. Serious inquiries only.

Spend Time with Me

Single black male, 35, caring, trustworthy, romantic, financially secure professional. Looking for single black female, honest, caring, affectionate, independent. No baggage, please.

Romeo Seeking Juliet

Single 25-year-old Hispanic male is seeking a single, physically fit Hispanic or black female, 20 to 26, who is open with her feelings. Must like some evenings out dining and dancing.

A Friend First

Early 40's, attractive, single Italian Hispanic female who likes outdoors and nature. Looking for handsome, single, nonsmoking, athletic male for friendship and possibly more.

Mature and Youthful

Male, 68, seeking a caring, outgoing, young-minded lady 55–65. I am educated and easy-going. I am looking for a long-term relationship.

There are also dating services that help people to meet people. The dating service asks customers to fill out a personal information form. It may ask

20 personal questions about **marital** status, children, education, religion, interests, occupation, income range, marriage attitude, smoking (smoker or nonsmoker), and drinking (social drinker or nondrinker). The form will also ask the same questions about the person that the customer is looking for. It could also include questions such as "What are the three most important things

25 you would look for in someone special?" Some dating services insist on meeting customers in person and may also require a **background check** conducted by an **external investigation agency.** The dating service then matches people according to the information given or gives the customers a **protected password** which enables them to search the service's **database** by

30 computer to find and select people they are interested in meeting. Some services also have customers make a video which will be shown to **prospective** matches. The customers then decide whom they would like to meet. Of course, there is a **fee** charged to customers for using a dating service.

Finally, there are chat rooms and **Web sites** on the Internet through

35 which a person can meet someone. (Many dating services also advertise on-line.) In chat rooms people send messages back and forth to get to know one another. People can **chat** with people of their own age, for example, 20s or 30s, or about a certain topic such as love and romance, parenting, music, politics, television programs, collecting things like books and autographs,

40 dolls and toys, antiques and art, to mention a few. People can also limit their chat to a specific geographic area such as Denver, Miami, or Chicago, if they wish. However, on the Internet geography is also no boundary, so people all over the world can chat with one another about different topics. In many chat programs people can choose to write **profiles** about themselves. The profiles

45 are available to all who know the screen name of the writers. After chatting over a period of time, some people decide to meet in person. In other cases chat room members will arrange to get a look at the people they are interested in meeting without them knowing it. The members locate the people through information given during the chatting and then go to places

50 where they can get a look at the people. If the members like what they see, they will then arrange to meet in person. If they do not, the chatting stops.

In addition, to find someone on the Internet, some people make up their own **Web sites** or **pages** on which they describe themselves and the type of person they are seeking. The description can include quite a few details. A

55 person can **browse** the Web sites and decide which person to contact.

With all these ways of finding a special person, newspaper advertisements, dating services, and the Internet, there should be no lonely people in the United States.

Sometimes there are bumps in the road to meeting that special someone.

GLOSSARY

actually (adv.) in fact; really

advertisement(s) (n.) A notice designed to attract public attention. **Ad(s)** is a short form of this word.

background check (n.) an examination of the information about a person to make sure that it is true

baggage (n.) Informal word meaning ideas, beliefs, or habits that influence the way a person acts

blind date (n.) a date between two people who have not previously met

database (n.) a collection of information (data) arranged for easy and speedy finding and reading (as on a computer)

external investigation agency (n.) a business that will do background checks on people at the request of another business

protected password (n.) a secret word or phrase that one uses to gain access to information (data) on a computer

QUICK COMPREHENSION CHECK

The paragraph on the next page is a brief summary of the selection's content. Read it carefully and complete the sentences with a word or phrase from the answer bank.

chat rooms	Internet	several
dating services	lonely	the United States
fee	meeting	Web sites
finding	newspaper advertisements	

In **(1)** _____ there are **(2)** _____

ways of **(3)** _____ a "special person" without actually

(4) _____ him or her. First is through **(5)** _____.

Second is through **(6)** _____. People must pay a

(7) _____ to use these. Finally, there are

(8) _____ and **(9)** _____ on

the **(10)** _____. With all these different ways, there

should be no **(11)** _____ people in this country.

QUESTIONS FOR THOUGHT AND DISCUSSION

1. What may be free when a person places a personal advertisement in the newspaper?

2. What will a person probably have to pay for?

3. What are two ways that a dating service could use to get people together?

4. What are two ways of meeting people on the Internet?

5. List the advantages and disadvantages for each of these ways of meeting people.

WAY	ADVANTAGES	DISADVANTAGES
Newspaper advertisements		
Dating service		
Chat room		
Web site		

6. Would you use one of these ways or would you want your son or daughter or other relative to use one of them? Why or why not?

7. What are some ways of meeting someone special that are not discussed in the selection?

8. Do you think that there are fewer lonely people in the United States than in other places because of these ways to locate partners? Why or why not?

ANOTHER LOOK AT THE SELECTION

You can do the following exercises in pairs or groups:

1. Read the sample advertisements again and list the words and expressions that describe (1) the person placing the ad and (2) the person who is being looked for. The first one is done for you as an example. Write any words that you are not sure of on the lines that follow. Can you get the meaning of the words from the context? Why or why not? Enter the words that you are teaching yourself in your **vocabulary log.**

ADVERTISEMENT	PERSON ONE	PERSON TWO
Seeking Serious Relationship	divorced	mature
	white	widowed
	with two children	divorced
	wants serious inquiries only	with children
		likes movies, playing sports, dinners at home

Words I am not sure of: _____

_____

_____

Words I am teaching myself: _____

_____

_____

ADVERTISEMENT	PERSON ONE	PERSON TWO
Spend Time with Me		
Romeo Seeking Juliet		
A Friend First		
Mature and Youthful		

Words I am not sure of : _____

_____

_____

Words I am teaching myself: _____

_____

_____

2. Write an advertisement of your own.

_____

_____

_____

_____

_____

_____

VOCABULARY BUILDING

Exercise 1: Match the following words or expressions from Selection 1 with their meanings. First scan the selection to find them. They are in bold print to help you find them easily. Examine the context and decide if you can understand the meaning from it. If you cannot, check the dictionary.

Vocabulary	Meanings
_____ **1.** assist (v.)	**a.** relating to marriage
_____ **2.** browse (v.)	**b.** a short biography
_____ **3.** chat (v.)	**c.** to commit something to the consideration of another
_____ **4.** fee (n.)	**d.** to talk in a relaxed, friendly, informal manner
_____ **5.** Internet (n.)	**e.** a place on the World Wide Web
_____ **6.** marital (adj.)	**f.** a charge or payment for a service
_____ **7.** profile (n.)	**g.** expected to happen
_____ **8.** prospective (adj.)	**h.** to help or aid
_____ **9.** retrieval (n.)	**i.** to look through something casually
_____ **10.** seek (v.)	**j.** to search for
_____ **11.** submit (v.)	**k.** the finding and reading of data (information)
_____ **12.** Web site (n.)	**l.** a worldwide network of computers

Exercise 2: Complete the sentences with the correct vocabulary from Exercise 1. You may have to change the form of some words.

1. Newspaper advertisements _____ people in finding that "special someone."

2. First a person must _____ the ad to the paper.

3. Usually there is free message _____, but a person must pay the telephone cost to _____ through the ads.

4. Dating services charge a _____ to help people find _____ partners.

5. The dating service will ask customers a number of questions about subjects such as current _____ status.

6. Another way to find a special person is through the _____.

7. People can _____ with other people and then decide if they want to meet them in person.

8. Many chat programs give members the choice to write a _____ of themselves.

9. People can also design their own _____ and on them give as much information about themselves as they want.

10. Many people in the U.S. _____ partners through the ways just described.

IN YOUR WORDS

Write a few sentences to answer each of the following questions:

1. Do people in your native land use newspaper advertisements, dating services, and the Internet to meet people? If yes, describe how they do it. If not, how do people meet "that special person" there? _____

_____

2. What advice would you give to a person who wanted to meet someone through the newspaper, a dating service, or the Internet? _____

_____

3. Which way do you think is the best way to meet someone special? Why?

_____

SUMMING UP

Share your answers to the questions above with the class.

1. Write a summary list of the answers given to first question above.

2. Summarize the advice the class would give to a person in the second question above.

3. Which way does the class think is the best way to meet someone special? Why? Which is the second-best way? Why?

READING JOURNAL

One way to become more involved in a reading selection is to keep a **reading journal** as you read. Use a notebook for your journal. Divide the notebook page in half lengthwise and make a two-column reading journal. At the top of the left-hand side write "What I Am Reacting To"; at the top of the right-hand side write "My Reaction." You can react to whatever you find in the reading selection: ideas, vocabulary, pictures, captions, unusual language. Your reaction can be an observation, a question, or a response of agreement, disagreement, surprise, anger, or frustration. Put into words what is going on in your head as you read.

As your read through the selection, answer the questions, do the exercises following the reading, and listen to class discussions, you may find the answers to all or some of the questions that you ask in your journal. If this happens, write the answers in the second column. Your journal can also help you participate more fully in class discussions because you will have your reactions in front of you.

One caution or warning: Do not make only vocabulary entries in your journal. Dig deeper and react to other things. Following are some sample entries for "Wanted: A bride. By next weekend." As you read the selection, refer to the sample entries and add your own.

READING JOURNAL

What I Am Reacting To	My Reaction
1. The title: "Wanted: A bride. By next weekend"	How can a person get a bride in a week?
2. bridal candidate mixer	What is this?
3. Paragraph 2 of the selection	Is this man crazy?
4. screen	What does it mean?

Keep a reading journal for Selections 2 and 3 in this chapter.

Selection 2A

DISCOVER WHAT YOU THINK

1. Do you think a person can decide to find "that special someone" in a set period of time? Why or why not?

_____

2. What do you think the title "Wanted: A bride. By next weekend" means?

_____

_____

The Tribune, Scranton, Pennsylvania, June 8, 1998

Wanted: A bride. By next weekend

Associated Press

MINNEAPOLIS—Only one thing is missing from Dave Weinlick's wedding plans: a bride.

The 28-year-old is getting married next Saturday. He has the rings, the minister, the musicians, his tuxedo and a reception all arranged. But he won't know who he'll meet at the altar until just before she walks down the aisle.

Potential brides are invited to attend Weinlick's "bridal candidate **mixer**" the day of the ceremony, where the groom's friends will **screen** them and their friends will **screen** Weinlick. There will be a vote, and Weinlick will marry the winner.

About four years ago, Weinlick got tired of people asking him when he

was going to get married, so he started to answer, "June 13, 1998." It became part of his **shtick**. At first he thought he might have a party to celebrate the idea of being in a **committed**,

Dave Weinlick, right, hands out invitations to his wedding and solicits possible candidates for his bride as he talks to Tess Schwanekamp at Calhoun Square in Minneapolis.

monogamous relationship, whether he was in one or not.

Then his friend and campaign coordinator Steve Fletcher suggested that he run a **campaign** and have a democratic wedding. As the date approached, the idea grew on him, and the campaign **got into full swing** about two months ago.

"The fact that this is not the norm is actually on my side," Weinlick said. "Somebody who is less likely to **go with the flow** is someone I'll be **compatible** with."

Weinlick, a graduate student in **anthropology** at the University of Minnesota, said that while he wants to keep his word about the wedding date, he also really wants to get married.

"I like the idea of being **committed** to someone and really

The Tribune, Scranton, Pennsylvania, June 8, 1998

making the relationship work," he said. "I think love develops. It's not just there."

Most of the **candidates** so far are people he knows, but there are a few he hasn't met face to face. And he hopes new ones surface.

Many have **entered the running** through his Bridal Nomination Committee Web site. Others have contacted Weinlick by phone.

Herman Weinlick, the groom's father, doesn't like the idea and plans **to skip** the wedding.

"I wish him well, and I admire his independence in many things,

> **Potential brides are invited to attend Weinlick's 'bridal candidate mixer' the day of the ceremony, where the groom's friends will screen them.**

including this," the elder Weinlick said. "But I am not particularly happy with this event, which I think **makes light of something** which, to me, should be taken more seriously."

Among his **attributes**, according to Fletcher: He's well-educated, has good credit and a clean record.

When asked if he is wealthy, Fletcher said Weinlick is "creatively wealthy" and has a "wealth of knowledge."

Matt Gundlach, a marriage and family counselor, says that while Weinlick's plan sounds like a great way to meet people, it doesn't sound like a **good bet** for a successful marriage.

"There's a **high probability** he's going to get the wrong person," he said. "I think usually with our friends, we pick who would be good for us, rather than what would be good for the other person.". . .

"Wanted: A Bride, by Next Weekend." Copyright © 1988. Reprinted by permission of the Associated Press.

GLOSSARY

enter the running (v.) to become a participant in something

get into full swing (v.) to become fully active

go with the flow (v.) to do the usual, normal thing

good bet (n.) a good chance of succeeding

make light of something (v.) to treat as unimportant

shtick (n.) a characteristic feature or trait that is helpful in securing recognition or attention (This word entered English from Yiddish, a language spoken by Jewish people chiefly in eastern Europe and areas to which they migrated.)

QUICK COMPREHENSION CHECK

Read the paragraph and complete the sentences with a word or phrase from the answer bank.

candidates	graduate student	vote
Dave	June 13, 1998	when he was getting married
democratic wedding	run a campaign	winner

David Weinlick is a (**1**) _____ at the University of Minnesota. He got tired of people asking (**2**) _____, so he started to answer (**3**) _____. His friend suggested that Dave (**4**) _____. As a result, on the day of the ceremony, Dave will have a (**5**) _____. Dave's friends will screen the (**6**) _____, and their friends will screen (**7**) _____. Then there will be a (**8**) _____, and Dave will marry the (**9**) _____.

QUESTIONS FOR THOUGHT AND DISCUSSION

1. How is David Weinlick going to find the woman he is going to marry?
2. Why did he decide to get married on June 13, 1998?
3. What was his first idea for June 13, 1998?
4. Where did he get the idea for his campaign to find a wife?
5. Who is David Weinlick?
6. What does he think about marriage and love?
7. How did he use the computer to help him?
8. In the article two people express their opinions about Dave's campaign to find a wife. Who expresses these opinions? What are the opinions? What support do the people give for their opinions?
9. What is your opinion of Dave's idea? Why?
10. Describe the type of woman, in your opinion, that would be a candidate in Dave's campaign.

ANOTHER LOOK AT THE SELECTION

You can do the following exercises in pairs or groups:

1. Herman Weinlick and Steve Fletcher use positive expressions to describe Dave Weinlick. What are these expressions?

   Herman Weinlick _____

   Steve Fletcher _____

2. Are any negative points about Dave Weinlick expressed by Herman Weinlick and Steve Fletcher?

Herman Weinlick _____

Steve Fletcher _____

3. In the following, which word is the **key** word? Does the word mean the same thing each time it is used? If not, what are the different meanings?

> When asked if he is wealthy, Fletcher said Weinlick is "creatively wealthy" and has a "wealth of knowledge."

4. How does Dave describe himself and the woman he hopes to find through his campaign?

5. What are some additional positive points made about Dave in the selection?

VOCABULARY BUILDING

Exercise 1: Match the following words or expressions from Selection 2 with their meanings.

Vocabulary

_____ **1.** anthropology (n.)

_____ **2.** attribute (n.)

_____ **3.** campaign (n.)

_____ **4.** candidate (n.)

_____ **5.** committed (adj.)

_____ **6.** compatible (adj.)

_____ **7.** high probability (n.)

_____ **8.** mixer (n.)

_____ **9.** monogamous (adj.)

_____ **10.** potential (adj.)

_____ **11.** screen (v.)

_____ **12.** skip (v.)

Meanings

a. to fail to attend

b. possible

c. being married to only one person at a time

d. quality or characteristic belonging to someone

e. capable of working or existing together

f. an informal party where people can meet

g. the scientific study of the origin, behavior, and physical, social, and cultural development of human beings

h. a person who seeks a position

i. to examine someone (or something) systematically to determine suitability

j. organized activity to reach a goal

k. very likely to happen

l. pledged, obliged

Exercise 2: Complete the sentences with the correct vocabulary from Exercise 1. You may have to change the form of some of the words.

1. Dave Weinlick, a graduate _____ student, decided to have his family and friends choose his bride for him.

2. He plans to have a _____ on the day of the wedding ceremony for the candidates.

3. The _____ brides will attend.

4. After family and friends _____ them, they will vote on the _____.

5. Steve Fletcher, Dave's friend, suggested the _____.

6. He feels that Dave has a number of positive _____.

7. Dave Weinlick seems to be _____ to a democratic wedding.

8. He says that he is looking for a _____ relationship.

9. Dave thinks that he and the wife he finds this way will be _____.

10. Dave's father is going to _____ the wedding.

11. Matt Gundlach, a marriage and family counselor, thinks there is a _____ that Dave will get the wrong person.

IN YOUR WORDS

Write a few sentences to answer each of the following questions:

1. What do you think is going to happen?

   _____

   _____

   _____

2. Would you recommend Dave's way of finding a person to marry? Why or why not?

   _____

   _____

   _____

3. What is your opinion of Dave Weinlick?

_____

_____

_____

_____

4. What is your opinion of the women who were candidates in his search?

_____

_____

_____

_____

SUMMING UP

Share your answers to the questions above.

1. As a class select the best answer to the first question above.

2. Write a summary statement of what the class thinks of Dave Weinlick.

_____

_____

3. Write a summary statement of what the class thinks of the women who were candidates.

_____

_____

4. Discuss your reading journals. Did they help you read more deeply? Were the questions that you asked in your journal answered during the discussion of the selection? If not, share these questions. Is there any comment from your journal that you would like to share with the class?

5. Remember to add at least five words to your vocabulary log.

Selection 2B

DISCOVER WHAT YOU THINK

1. Describe what you think Dave Weinlick's bride is like?

_____

2. What is a "megamall"? Do you think people should get married in one? Why or why not?

_____

_____

The Tribune, Scranton, Pennsylvania, June 14, 1998

After Friends Pick Bride, Pair Marries at Megamall

Associated Press

BLOOMINGTON, Minn.—David Weinlick had known for years that he wanted to get married Saturday. He knew where the wedding would be held and who the guests would be. He just hadn't picked out a bride.

A couple of dozen adventurous women from several states showed up Saturday at a "bridal candidate mixer" to **brave** questioning by Weinlick's friends and relatives, whose votes **determined** that Elizabeth Runze would be his bride.

Soon after the selection, the two 28-year-olds exchanged vows at the **Mall of America**. About 2,000 shoppers lined the **rails** to watch from the three upper levels of the mall's **rotunda**.

Runze, a slender redhead, wore a short-sleeved white dress with a full

Elizabeth Runze looks up as David Weinlick says "I do" during their wedding in Bloomington, Minn. His family and friends picked her from 23 possible brides less than two hours earlier.

skirt and a fitted **bodice** embroidered with flowers, a short veil and elbow-length gloves. Her father walked her down the aisle and her parents, who are divorced, **gave her away**. The groom wore a black tuxedo.

A minister friend of Weinlick's conducted the brief ceremony. Balloons fell from the ceiling and the crowd cheered as the couple kissed.

"I can hardly stand [up] much less talk," Runze, a **pharmacy** student at the University of Minnesota, said shortly after she was selected. "This is the most incredible day of my life."

Before the wedding, Weinlick said he was **"elated"** and called the event "an enormous success." "This is almost exactly what I could have hoped for," he said.

Weinlick's friend Steven Fletcher said the two had similar interests and

The Tribune, Scranton, Pennsylvania, June 14, 1998

senses of humor and were a good **fit** intellectually.

"You can see the **chemistry between these two,**" he said. "Those two just look right together."

Annette Runze said her daughter talked to Weinlick, a tall thin blond who sports a ponytail, for the first time Monday when she dropped off her application. She said she and Elizabeth's father support the marriage.

"She's very serious about it. She's very committed to the idea and so is he. They'll probably be married for 67 years."

The four finalists, two from Minnesota, one from Florida and one who refused to give her hometown, were among the five bridesmaids.

Weinlick is a graduate student in anthropology, and his marriage plan **played out** like some sort of weird social experiment.

Four years ago, Weinlick said, he grew tired of being asked when he was going to get married, so he came up with a **stock** answer: June 13, 1998.

With the **deadline** upon him Saturday, friends and relatives interviewed the candidates.

"The first question I always ask is, 'Why should I let you marry our Dave?'" said Kathi Diehl, a friend of eight years from Omaha, Nebraska.

Weinlick's sister, Wenonah Wilms of Minneapolis, said all of the candidates were nice but she was looking for something more.

"I'm picking a sister-in-law," Wilms said. "I have to pick someone who is going to be there at Christmas."

The suggestion that Weinlick try love democratic style and let his **pals** pick the bride came from his friend, Fletcher.

"After Friends Pick Bride, Pair Marries at Megamall." Copyright © 1988. Reprinted by permission of the Associated Press.

GLOSSARY

bodice (n.) the fitted upper part of a dress

brave (v.) to undergo or face something with courage

chemistry between two people (n.) mutual attraction

Mall of America (name) the largest mall in the United States; located in Bloomington, Minnesota

rail (n.) horizontal bar used as a barrier

rotunda (n.) a round room or building, especially one with a dome

stock (adj.) repeated often without any thought as in "a stock answer"

QUICK COMPREHENSION CHECK

Complete the sentences with a word or phrase from the answer bank below.

chose	Mall of America	selected
elated	Minnesota	28
Elizabeth Runze	pharmacy major	the University of Minnesota

Dave Weinlick married **(1)** _____ at the

(2) _____ in **(3)** _____. She

is a **(4)** _____ at **(5)** _____.

They are both **(6)** _____ years old. Dave's family

and friends **(7)** _____ four finalists and then

(8) _____ the slender redhead. Weinlick was

(9) _____.

QUESTIONS FOR THOUGHT AND DISCUSSION

1. How many women appeared at the bridal candidate mixer?

2. Describe the woman chosen to be Dave Weinlick's bride.

3. What was Dave's opinion of the wedding?

4. Describe the bride on the day of her wedding.

5. What did Steven Fletcher think of the couple?

6. What did the bride's mother and father think of the marriage?

7. What was the bride's attitude toward the marriage?

8. What was the first question that Dave's friend Kathi Diehl asked candidates? Do you think that this was a good question? Why or why not?

9. What do you think that Dave's sister Wenonah Wilms meant when she said that all the candidates were nice but she was looking for something more?

10. What do you think of the bride?

11. Would you call the search for the bride a success? Why or why not?

12. Do you think the marriage will be a success? Why or why not?

ANOTHER LOOK AT THE SELECTION

You can do the following exercises in pairs or groups:

1. Describe the wedding by writing a few sentences about each of the following:

Groom _____

_____

_____

Bride _____

_____

_____

Bridesmaids _____

_____

_____

Ceremony _____

_____

_____

Guests/Observers _____

_____

_____

2. Steven Fletcher, Dave Weinlick's friend, uses positive expressions to describe Dave and his bride. What are they?

_____

3. What expressions does Annette Runze, the mother of the bride, use to describe her daughter and her daughter's attitude toward the marriage?

_____

VOCABULARY BUILDING

Exercise 1: Match the following words or expressions from Selection 2 with their meanings.

Vocabulary

_____ **1.** deadline (n.)

_____ **2.** determine (v.)

_____ **3.** elated (adj.)

_____ **4.** fit (n.)

_____ **5.** to give someone away (v.)

_____ **6.** pal (n.)

_____ **7.** pharmacy (adj.; n.)

_____ **8.** to play out (v.)

_____ **9.** sense of humor (n.)

Meanings

a. a friend (informal)

b. joyful; happy; in high spirits

c. an ability to understand or appreciate something funny or comical

d. match

e. the study and profession of preparing and dispensing drugs

f. settle or decide something firmly and conclusively

g. a set time by which something must be finished

h. present a bride to the groom in a marriage ceremony

i. finish

Exercise 2: Complete the sentences with the correct vocabulary from Exercise 1. You may have to change the form of some words. One word is not used.

1. On the day of his wedding Dave Weinlick was _____.

2. His friends and relatives cast votes which _____ that a slender redhead, Elizabeth Runze, would be his bride.

3. She is a student of _____ at the University of Minnesota.

4. Her parents _____ during the wedding ceremony.

5. Dave's friend, Steven Fletcher, thinks that the couple is a good _____.

6. Each of them has a good _____, which is very important in married life.

7. Dave's campaign to find a bride _____ as he wanted.

8. In the end, Dave met his _____ of being married by June 13, 1998.

IN YOUR WORDS

Write a few sentences to answer each of the following questions:

1. What is your opinion of the wedding ceremony?

_____

_____

_____

2. What is your prediction for the future of this marriage?

_____

_____

_____

3. What advice would you give to the newly married couple?

_____

_____

_____

SUMMING UP

Share your answers to the following:

1. Which selection was easier to read, Selection 2A or 2B? Why?

2. What fact or facts in Selections 2A and 2B surprised you the most?

3. If you were asked to vote to choose someone's husband or wife, would you do it? Why or why not?

4. Discuss your reading journals with the class. Were the questions that you asked in your journal answered during the discussion of the selection? If not, share these questions. Is there any comment from your journal that you would like to share with the class?

5. Remember to add at least five new words to your vocabulary log.

Selection 3

DISCOVER YOURSELF

1. What do you think "The Sunshine of My Life" means?

_____

_____

2. Freewrite about a person whom you would call "The Sunshine of My Life." Continue writing until your teacher tells you to stop.

THE SUNSHINE OF MY LIFE

It is Friday. Tomorrow my husband Jarek will be back home from his trip to his Uncle Jan in Chicago. It is the first time and the last time I will let him go anywhere without me. I did not think that I **would miss** him so much. It has been a long week without him. I **miss** his jokes about my hair color, and I miss his smile, his voice. But what can I do now? The only thing I can do is to call him and keep waiting for him.

I remember the first time I met him. It was exactly one month after I came to the United States on September 18, 1993. I even remember the time! It was 6:15 P.M. I was waiting for my friend Ania near St. Stanislaw Roman Catholic Church in Greenpoint, Brooklyn, where I was living. My husband was working in that church at that time. Ania, as usual, was late. I was ready to give up and go home, when HE came. All I remember from this moment is his warm, sunny smile. Now I know that he smiles like that to everybody, but then I believed it was only for me. Because he had a couple of minutes, we started to talk. Before he left, he gave me his phone number. On the next day I called him and we set our first date.

We did not **fall in love** at once. It was a long process. At first, I liked the way he looked, dressed, and talked, but it was not love. Jarek has beautiful blue eyes and long dark lashes. Looking into his eyes is like looking at Morskie Oko, a beautiful lake surrounded by pine trees in the Tatry Mountains in Poland. That is what impressed me the most at the beginning. Also, I have always liked tall men. Jarek is over six feet tall, and that was an additional "point" for him at the beginning of our **acquaintance.** He is a **good-looking** man. Sometimes I tell him that he looks like one of the Greek

25 gods. I think that he does not even realize that he has an attractive athletic body or that he is handsome.

That is what was important to me at the beginning. Later on I started to love 30 not only his appearance but also his personality. He was always very **understanding.** I did not have much time for him and he never complained. I had to work during the day, and in the 35 evenings I was taking English classes. At that time I was working in a factory in Brooklyn. I worked ten hours a day, and sometimes when I got home I did not want to go to school. I used to call Jarek 40 before I went to school, and whenever I did not want to go, he made me do it. He would **make fun of me,** that I just loved my work, and I did not need anything better from life because what 45 I had was enough to make me happy. I would get mad at him for not understanding, but . . . I would go to school.

Morskie Oko,
Tatry Mountains, Poland

Whenever I had any problem, Jarek, like a good friend, was always ready to help me. Once I had to stay late at work. When I left, it was already 50 11:00 P.M. I was very scared and I did not want to take the subway. While I was waiting for a cab, I called Jarek. I didn't know he was sleeping so I woke him up. I said I was very sorry but he said that it was not a problem, and even more, he came to pick me up. At that time I realized that I **meant something to him.**

55 Jarek is not an **outgoing** person. He has a couple of friends, but most of his time he likes to spend at home or alone. I realized it soon after I met him. On my first Christmas in the new country it was proved. At that time, I had known Jarek for four months, and we had become a couple of good friends. Our relationship was not "exclusive" yet, but we liked to be together. On 60 Christmas Eve we were invited for dinner by one of his friends, but we decided to spend that evening alone in Jarek's place. Actually it was his decision. He lived alone in a one-bedroom apartment while I shared one little room with my friend. I was tired of being with people all the time and was glad that we were going to be alone. After work I went to his apartment, 65 and I was supposed to cook traditional Christmas Eve dinner. I tried hard to

Malgorzata Kaczynski at Christmas

impress him, but at that time I was not a good cook. From the five dishes I made, only one was **edible.** We **were starving,** and finally Jarek **saved the day** and made hot dogs. I will remember those hot dogs forever.

After that Christmas we started to spend more and more time together, and finally we could not even go shopping one without the other. After work I used to go directly to Jarek's place where I stayed until late at night. Jarek wanted me to live with him, but I did not want to. First of all, we **were** not **married.** I was not even sure if I wanted **to marry him.** Another thing was that I wanted to be his girlfriend and be with him all the time, but I also wanted to have a place where I could be without him. I was very confused. I just did not know what I wanted. I did not know that I loved Jarek.

I loved Jarek, but it took me the next six months to realize it. In May (five months after our first Christmas) Jarek went to Poland for three weeks to visit his parents. At first, when he left, I felt free. I was glad that I could have so much time for myself. During the first week of this "vacation," I shopped, visited friends, and had fun, but then I started **to miss him.** I called him almost every day and I wanted him to come back. I think at that time I found out that I loved him.

Two weeks after he came back from Poland we **got married.** Now we are a very happy couple. Our love is growing, and every day life always brings something new. Even though we **have been married** for over two years, I still find something in my husband that surprises me, something that I did not know about before. I love him more and more every day. He is the sunshine of my life.

Malgorzata Kaczynski
Poland

QUICK COMPREHENSION CHECK

Complete the sentences with a word or phrase from the answer bank. Remember to preview the sentences in the exercise before you read.

at once	his smile	some time
called	Jarek	two years
church	Malgorzata	very happy
her problems	she loved him	went on a date

(1) _____ met (2) _____ in front of a (3) _____. The only thing she remembers from the meeting was (4) _____. The next day she (5) _____ him, and they (6) _____. She did not fall in love (7) _____. He helped her with (8) _____. It took her (9) _____ to realize that (10) _____. They have been married for (11) _____, and she is (12) _____. He is the sunshine of her life.

QUESTIONS FOR THOUGHT AND DISCUSSION

1. Describe how Malgorzata met Jarek the first time.
2. Who made the first telephone call after the first meeting? What do you think about this?
3. At first, what attracted her to him? What details does she give to describe this attraction?
4. Later on, what attracted her? What examples does she give to illustrate this attraction?
5. Describe what happened on Christmas Eve. What happened with the food?
6. When did Malgorzata realize that she loved Jarek?
7. How did she feel when he went to visit his family?
8. When did she marry him?
9. How does Malgorzata feel two years after her marriage to Jarek?

10. What does Jarek feel about Malgorzata? Support your position with lines from the selection.

11. What is your prediction for the future of Malgorzata and Jarek? Why?

ANOTHER LOOK AT THE SELECTION

You can do the following exercises in pairs or groups:

1. Malgorzata uses many positive expressions to describe Jarek. List at least five of these expressions.

2. List the negative expressions that she uses to describe Jarek. What is the difference between the positive and negative expressions? Why is there this difference?

3. Malgorzata uses word pictures to describe Jarek. Word pictures help the reader to see what is in the writer's mind. For example, Malgorzata writes, "Sometimes I tell him that he looks like one of the Greek gods." What does this word picture make you think about Jarek? Find another word picture that she uses in her description of Jarek. What does this word picture make you think about him?

4. List the details that Malgorzata gives which help the reader experience the Christmas Eve dinner.

5. In paragraph six in the selection Malgorzata says, "I was very confused. I just did not know what I wanted." What examples does she give to illustrate her confusion?

VOCABULARY BUILDING

VOCABULARY STRATEGY:
A way to build your vocabulary is to learn some of the common prefixes used in English. A prefix is a syllable placed at the beginning of a word to change its meaning. You have already seen words with prefixes in the reading selections in Chapters 1 and 2. Examples are *superman, superheroine, monogamous,* and *megamall.* Following is one half of a list of common prefixes and their meanings with some vocabulary samples. Since the list is so long, the other half will be given in Chapter 3. Use prefixes to help you figure out the meanings of words. Enter the prefixes that are new to you or that you are not sure of in your **vocabulary log.**

PREFIX	MEANING	SAMPLE WORDS
ante-	Prior to, earlier	antedate, antecedent
anti- (ant- before a,e,i,o,u)	Against	antiwar, antacid
auto-	Self Automatic	autobiography, autoimmune autopilot
bi-	Two Both sides, parts, directions At intervals of two Twice during (a month)	bifocals bilateral bicentennial bimonthly
com-	Together, with	combine, compete
contra-	Against, opposite	contradiction, contraception
cyber-	Computer Computer network	cyberphobia cyberculture
de-	From, off, apart, away, down, out Reversal, removal, reduction	deactivate, decontaminate
dis-	Not, not any	disbelieve, disrespect
equi-	Equal, equally	equidistant, equivalent
ex- ex- (with hyphen)	Out, from Former	exit, extend ex-wife, ex-President
fore-	Before, in front	forerunner, forefront
geo-	Earth Geography	geography geomagnetism, geopolitics
il-, im-, in-, ir-, un-	Not	illegal, illogical, imbalanced, impossible, inactive, irregular, irrelevant, unhappy, unhealthy

PREFIX	MEANING	SAMPLE WORDS
mega-	One million Large	megabyte, megawatt megaphone, megamall
micro- **(opposite of macro-)**	Small Large	microchip, microfilm, microcosm macrocosm
mid-	Middle	midmorning, midyear mid-November, mid-Atlantic (note the use of the hyphen with a word that begins with a capital letter)
mis-	Bad, badly Wrong, wrongly	misfortune, misbehave misspelling, misunderstand
mono-	One, only, single	monogamous, monochromatic
multi-	Many More than two Many times over	multicolored, multinational multiracial multimillionaire

Exercise 1: Use the vocabulary in the following list to complete the sentences. Use the sentence context to help choose the correct word. You may have to change the form of some of the words.

autobiography	decontaminate	geopolitics	microchip
bifocals	ex-wife	irrelevant	misbehave
bimonthly	forefront	megabyte	monochromatic

1. I can't see anything far away and I can't see anything that is close, so I must get a pair of _____.

2. His _____ wants complete custody of the children as well as a lot of alimony.

3. The neighbor gave the police many details about the suspect, but most of them were really _____.

4. How many _____ does your computer have?

5. The doctor's medical discovery put him at the _____ of his profession.

6. Many towns are now trying to _____ land on which there had been factories that made poisonous chemicals.

7. Since the painter only liked the color green, all of his works of art were

_____.

8. The student workers at the university are all paid _____.

9. The child _____ in the mall, so her mother told her that she could not have any ice cream.

10. If a person writes a book about his or her life, it is called an

_____.

11. As developments in technology have continued, the _____ in computers have grown smaller and smaller.

12. Since my son has always like geography and politics, he has decided to major in _____.

Exercise 2: Match the following words or expressions from Selection 3 with their meanings:

Vocabulary

_____ **1.** acquaintance (n.)

_____ **2.** edible (adj.)

_____ **3.** fall in love (v.)

_____ **4.** good-looking (adj.)

_____ **5.** impress (v.)

_____ **6.** make fun of someone/something (v.)

_____ **7.** mean something to someone (v.)

_____ **8.** miss someone/something (v.)

_____ **9.** outgoing (adj.)

_____ **10.** save the day (v.)

_____ **11.** starve (v.)

_____ **12.** understanding (adj.)

Meanings

a. compassionate; sympathetic

b. friendly; sociable

c. to be hungry (informal)

d. to have a strong, often favorable effect on the mind or feelings of somebody

e. fit to be eaten

f. to prevent a misfortune

g. become enamored or inspired with love

h. to ridicule; mock

i. having a pleasing appearance; attractive

j. to feel the absence of someone or something

k. to be of importance

l. relationship less close than friendship

Exercise 3: Complete the sentences with the correct vocabulary from Exercise 2. You may have to change the form of some of the words.

1. It took Malgorzata some time to _____ with Jarek.

2. When she first saw him, she thought that he was very _____.

3. At the beginning of their _____ she was attracted to him physically.

4. Later on she found that he did not have an _____ personality.

5. But Jarek _____ her with his _____ ways.

6. When she did not want to go to class, he _____ of her and she went.

7. Their first Christmas together she cooked only one _____ dish.

8. She will never forget that holiday because Jarek _____ by making hot dogs.

9. Before dinner they _____, so they will never forget those Christmas hot dogs!

10. When Jarek took a trip to Poland to visit his family, she _____ him very much.

11. She discovered that he _____ very special to her.

Exercise 4: The following vocabulary words are commonly used when talking or writing about the topic of marriage. Use the correct form in the blanks. Which two expressions can be used in the same blank? Can these two expressions always be used interchangeably?

marriage (n.)   marry (v.)   to be married (v.)   to get married (v.)

   I am going _____ next month. It has taken me a long time to decide _____ my boyfriend. _____ is a very serious step and should be entered into with great care. I intend _____ to the same person for the rest of my life.

IN YOUR WORDS

Write your answers to the following questions:

1. What is your favorite part of the selection and why?

_____

_____

_____

_____

_____

_____

2. Write a list of at least eight positive expressions that describe "the sunshine of your life."

_____

_____

_____

_____

_____

_____

_____

_____

_____

3. Write two word pictures that describe "the sunshine of your life."

_____

_____

_____

_____

_____

_____

_____

_____

_____

_____

SUMMING UP

Share your answers to the questions above with a partner or group members.

1. Did any members choose the same part of the selection? If so, which one(s)?

2. Share the lists of positive expressions. Add new ones to your own list.

3. Share your word pictures. Is there any one that the group liked the best?

4. Discuss your reading journals with the class. Were the questions that you asked in your journal answered during the discussion of the selection? If not, share these questions. Is there any comment from your journal that you would like to share with the class?

5. Remember to add at least five new words to your vocabulary log.

REFLECTING AND SYNTHESIZING

A. Share your vocabulary log and reading journal with a partner or group. Have all the questions in your reading journal been answered? If not, discuss them with your partner or the group. Can you make any additional entries in your vocabulary log? Are the vocabulary logs helping you to build your vocabulary? Why or why not?

B. After answering the following, share your thoughts with your partner, group, or class.

    1. Which selection did you like the best? Why?

    2. Reflect on the four reading selections. From your reflection make at least one observation about meeting that special someone.

    3. Write about the best way to meet a special person in the culture that you came from.

    4. Give advice to someone who wants to meet a special person in the United States.

C. Answer these questions on your own.

    1. Write about how you met a special person.

    2. Did your ideas about meeting someone special change as a result of the material in this chapter? If Yes, how? If No, why not? What did you think before you read the chapter and what do you think now?

    3. Describe "the sunshine" of your life.

    4. Write your definition of "happy love."

    5. Describe the perfect special someone for you.

    6. Describe the perfect wedding ceremony.

...How the Work Force Is Changing

A SNAPSHOT OF SHIFTING DEMAND

Goodbye, coal-mining and factory work. Hello, retailing and health care. Better go job-hunting at a smaller company, too.

PERCENTAGE OF EMPLOYEES BY INDUSTRY

```
80%
60          Service
40          Goods
20
 0
 1970  80   90  97
```

EMPLOYEES, IN MILLIONS, IN COMPANIES OF:

```
100   Fewer than 499
 80    employees
 60
 40   500 employees
 20    or more
  0
 1980  85   90   95
```

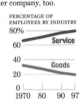

PERCENTAGE OF MARRIED WOMEN IN THE LABOR FORCE WITH CHILDREN UNDER 6 YEARS OLD

```
80%
60
40
20
 0
1960 70  80  90 97
```

THE VIEW FOR THE BEGINNERS

Small wonder no one has time for truth and beauty in college anymore. The 1998 stats reveal some pretty career-minded kids.

FRESHMEN DECLARING MAJORS

Business	16.5%
Education	11.8
Health professional	11.1
Other nontechnical	9.1
Other technical	8.2
Engineering	8.2
Undecided	7.5
Social science	6.4
Biological science	5.6

STARTING SALARIES BY STUDENT MAJORS

Chemical engineering	$45,104
Electrical engineering	43,282
Computer science	41,949
Accounting	32,825
Business administration	31,454
History	26,820
English and literature	26,300
Psychology	25,689

STARTING SALARY OF ENTRY-LEVEL POSITIONS

Software developer	$43,415
Consultant	39,969
Investment banker	37,120
Sales	30,270
Brand/product manager	30,036
HR/Industrial relations	27,634

92% of job seekers off found jobs better salaries in 1998

28% of all full-time workers had flexible work schedule compared with 12% in 1985

8 million people held down more than one job in 1997 compared with 3.8 million multiple-job holders in 1965

10.5 million workers were self-employed in 1997 compared with 7 million workers in 1970

26% of the workers in a recent survey had been in their current job for 12 months or less; 15% had been in the same job for 3 to 4 years

3% of the nation's college freshmen indicated interest in a law career in 1998—the lowest number ever

SOURCES: BU
CHALLENG
RESEARC
GRAPHI

3

GOING FORWARD: EDUCATION AND EMPLOYMENT

OPENING THOUGHT

Hitch your wagon to a star.

Ralph Waldo Emerson (1803–1882), United States

Take a few minutes to think about the quotation that introduces this chapter. Answer the following questions:

1. What do you think this quotation means?

_____

_____

_____

_____

2. Do you think people should "hitch their wagons to stars"? Why or why not?

_____

_____

_____

_____

3. Give some examples of how to do this.

_____

_____

_____

_____

Share your thoughts with your partner, group, or class.

Selection 1

DISCOVER WHAT YOU KNOW

1. Why do people attend a college or university in the United States?

_____

_____

_____

_____

2. Why are you attending a college or university now?

_____

_____

_____

3. Do you think students should have an open mind when they attend a college or university? Why or why not?

_____

_____

_____

_____

_____

_____

USING THE UNIVERSITY [OR COLLEGE] TO ACHIEVE

How Open Am I to the Challenge of the University [or College]?

What is the **challenge** of the university [or college]? When it is best understood, the challenge of the university [or college] **reveals** itself more as an opportunity than a contest between **adversaries.** It is an opportunity for each student to earn an education by challenging himself or herself to meet

5 the standards set by the university [or college] in a range of academic programs. Successfully meeting this challenge moves the student closer to achieving his or her goals, which

10 include those career, citizen, and individual goals designated by the university. And, it is the student who is more open to the challenge who more likely will succeed.

15 How can a student know when he or she is open? Are there useful **indicators** of openness? Let openness refer to those student behaviors that demonstrate the ability and willingness to (1) give

20 **critical** and **rational** consideration (not necessarily acceptance) to ideas and values that differ from their own, even when those ideas and values push the students to the edges of their **comfort zone,** (2) give a critical look at their

25 own **core** beliefs and values, which are often culture based, (3) demonstrate a reasonable **tolerance** for uncertainty, that is, do not need to have an answer for everything, all the time, and (4) risk and accept being wrong, while learning from mistakes.

Indeed, this capacity for openness seems to be **essential** for meeting the

30 challenge of the university [or college]. Also, the sense of adventure and curiosity that is an important part of openness permits the student to enjoy that challenge.

Reprinted from *Your Key to Success,* Kean University, edited by Christopher Lynch. Copyright © 1998 by Simon & Schuster Custom Publishing. All rights reserved. Reprinted by permission from Pearson Custom Publishing, Boston, MA.

GLOSSARY

comfort zone (n. phrase) a belief structure in which a person feels at ease, not threatened

essential (adj.) very important, necessary

QUICK COMPREHENSION CHECK

Complete the sentences, using words from the answer bank.

contest	goals
enjoy	open
essential	opportunity
four	standards

The challenge of a university [or college] is more of an **(1)** _____ for students than a **(2)** _____ between the students and the university [or college]. The students challenge themselves to meet the **(3)** _____ set by the university. Successfully meeting this challenge moves the students closer to meeting their own **(4)** _____. It is the student who is more **(5)** _____ who will more likely succeed. The selection presents **(6)** _____ indicators of openness. The capacity for openness seems to be **(7)** _____ to meeting the challenge of a university [or college]. Also the sense of adventure and curiosity that is a part of openness permits the student to **(8)** _____ the challenge.

QUESTIONS FOR THOUGHT AND DISCUSSION

1. What is the challenge of the university or college?
2. What happens when the student successfully meets the challenge?
3. What kind of student will most likely succeed?
4. What is a "comfort zone"? What may happen to a student's comfort zone in the first indicator of openness?
5. In the second indicator what do students examine?

6. What is "a reasonable tolerance for uncertainty"?

7. What is the fourth indicator of openness?

8. According to the selection, how important is the capacity for openness?

9. Can students enjoy the challenge of a university or college? Why or why not?

ANOTHER LOOK AT THE SELECTION

1. Read the four indicators of openness described in the selection again. On the following lines, restate them in your own words:

_____

_____

_____

_____

_____

2. Select one of the indicators above and give an example of it.

_____

_____

_____

_____

VOCABULARY BUILDING

VOCABULARY STRATEGY (continued from Chapter 2):
What is a prefix? _____
How can prefixes help your vocabulary building? _____
_____

The list of prefixes begun in Chapter 2 continues below. Enter the ones that are new to you or that you are not sure of in your **vocabulary log.**

PREFIX	MEANING	SAMPLE WORDS
non-	Not	nonsense, nonessential, nonstop, nonviolence
omni-	All	omnipotent, omnipurpose, omnipresent
out-	Outside of Stands out and above others Doing better or being greater	outbuilding, outcast outstanding outdo, outnumber, outrun
post-	After	postdate, postnatal, postwar
pre-	Earlier, before In advance	prehistory prepay
pro **pro- with hyphen**	Favoring, supporting Before or earlier	proslavery, prowar prologue pro-French, pro-American
re-	Again	rebuild, recall, redo, remake, rewrite
self-	Indicates something about oneself	self-employed, self-improvement
sub-	Under Less than completely	subway, subsoil subhuman, substandard
super-	Above, over, upon Superior in size, quality, number, or degree Exceeding a standard or norm Excessive in degree or intensity	superimpose superman, superhuman supersonic supersensitive
ultra-	Beyond the range, limit, normal degree of	ultrasound, ultraviolet
un-	Not	unfeeling, unequal, uncertainty
under-	Position beneath or below Incompleteness, or falling below a certain standard	underarm, undershirt, undercurrent underdeveloped, underfeed, underestimate
uni-	One	unicorn, unison, unilateral
zoo-	Animal, living being	zoology

Exercise 1: Use the vocabulary in the following list to fill in the blanks in the sentences. Use the sentence context to help choose the correct word. You may have to change the form of some of the words.

nonessential	rebuild	undercurrent
omnipotent	substandard	underfeed
omnipresent	supersensitive	zoology
outbuilding	ultrasound	
prepay	uncertainty	

1. After the earthquake the people in the country had to decide whether or not to _____ their houses in the same place.

2. Ana, who is _____, will cry if you look at her in the wrong way.

3. The travel agent told us that we had to _____ all of our hotels before we went on the trip.

4. Some people _____ their dogs because they do not want them to get fat.

5. The financial planner told the couple that, if they wanted to save money, they would have to eliminate all _____ purchases from their lives.

6. When people decide to emigrate to another country, they know that they will face much _____.

7. The owner of the store decided that he would not sell _____ merchandise.

8. Cheng Yen always loved animals, so it is not surprising that she chose to major in _____.

9. The country estate had one large residence and six _____ of different kinds including a garage, a barn, a stable, and three sheds.

10. In a number of religions, God is said to be _____ and _____.

11. There was an _____ of dissatisfaction in the country because of the poor performance of the elected leaders.

12. The patient is having an echocardiogram, which means looking at the heart using _____.

Exercise 2: Match the following words or expressions from Selection 1 with their meanings. First, scan the selection to find them. They are in bold print to help you find them easily. Examine the context and decide if you can understand the meaning from it. If you cannot, check the dictionary.

Vocabulary

_____ **1.** adversary (n.)

_____ **2.** challenge (n.)

_____ **3.** core (adj.)

_____ **4.** critical (adj.)

_____ **5.** indicator (n.)

_____ **6.** rational (adj.)

_____ **7.** reveal (v.)

_____ **8.** tolerance (n.)

Meanings

a. basic; most important part

b. something that serves as a sign

c. an opponent or enemy

d. ability to endure

e. something that tests a person's skills, efforts, or resources

f. based on reason; logical

g. showing careful judgment

h. to make something clear or easier to understand

Exercise 3: Fill in the blanks with the correct vocabulary from Exercise 2. You may have to change the form of some words.

1. The challenge of the university should not be thought of as a contest between _____.

2. There are several _____ that _____ a student's capacity for openness.

3. Students must give critical and _____ consideration to ideas and values different from their own.

4. They must give a _____ look at their own _____ beliefs and values.

5. They must show a reasonable _____ for uncertainty and risk and accept being wrong while learning from their mistakes.

6. The capacity for openness seems to be essential for meeting the _____ of the university [or college].

IN YOUR WORDS

Answer the following in a few sentences:

1. Do you agree that a student who is more open is more likely to succeed in a college or university? Why or why not?

_____

_____

_____

_____

_____

2. Give an example from your own experience or observation of becoming more "open" while attending college or university.

_____

_____

_____

_____

_____

SUMMING UP

Now share your answers with the class.

1. In a few sentences, summarize the answers of the class to number 1 above.

2. Which examples from number 2 above did the class find most interesting?

3. Have the questions in your reading journal been answered?

4. Remember to make your entries in your vocabulary log.

Selection 2

DISCOVER WHAT YOU THINK

1. Have you ever been on a job interview? Was it a positive or negative experience? Why?

_____

_____

_____

2. What kind of employment would you like to find after graduation?

_____

_____

_____

3. How important do you think that the personal interview is in a job search? Why?

_____

_____

NEXT TIME, EAT THE PIZZA AFTER THE INTERVIEW

Clean your fingernails. Make sure no food is stuck between your teeth. Polish your shoes. And your résumé.

For years, **self-help books** have been **preaching** these basic rules for job interviews. Getting in the door is a good start, of course. It's your chance to
5 separate yourself from that stack of applications, to impress the boss with all your personal charm. The goal isn't just getting in the door, though. It's leaving with a job.

But some **sad sacks** never **get the word.** A survey of personnel executives at 200 of the **Fortune 1000 companies** turned up a wide range of
10 strange and **self-defeating** behavior by some applicants about a year ago. The results are a **primer** on what not to do on a job interview.

The survey was conducted for Commemorative Brands, a manufacturer of high school and college class rings, by the New York research firm Schulman, Ronca and Bucuvalas. Here is a sampling of comments from the interviewers:

- "The reason the candidate was taking so long to respond to a question became apparent when he began to **snore**."

- "During the entire interview, the applicant wore a baseball cap. . . . A few days later another college graduate showed up for a **management trainee position** wearing **overalls** and sandals."

- "When I asked the candidate to give a good example of the organizational skills she **was boasting about,** she said she was proud of her ability to pack her suitcase 'real neat' for her vacations."

- "Wanted to know if employee **perks** included a swimming pool, paid lunches at the company cafeteria or a free computer to use at home."

- "Why did he go to college? His **ill-conceived** answer: 'To party and socialize.'"

- "He couldn't answer any of my questions because he had just had major dental work."

- "When I gave him my business card at the beginning of the interview, he immediately **crumpled** it and **tossed** it into the wastebasket."

- "I received a résumé and a note that said the recent high school graduate wanted to earn $25 an hour—'and not a nickel less.'"

- "He had arranged for a pizza to be delivered to my office during a lunch-hour interview. I asked him not to eat it until later."

- "Said she had just graduated cum laude, but had no idea what cum laude meant. However, she was proud of her grade point average. It was 2.1."

- "Insisted on telling me that he wasn't afraid of hard work. But insisted on adding that he was afraid of horses and didn't like jazz, modern art or seafood."

- "The candidate never looked directly at me once during the entire interview. Just **stared** at the floor."

45
- "An otherwise qualified candidate **took herself out of the running** when she opened her mouth. She had her tongue pierced."

50
- "She actually showed up for an interview during the summer wearing a bathing suit. She said she didn't think I'd **mind.**"

55
- "He sat down opposite me, made himself comfortable and proceeded to put his foot up on my desk."

60
- "The interview had gone well, until he told me that he and his friends wore my company's clothing. At which point, I had to tell him that we manufactured office products, not

65
sportswear."

- "Applied for a customer service position although, as he confided, he really

70
wasn't a people person."

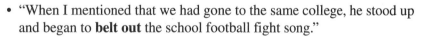

- "When I mentioned that we had gone to the same college, he stood up and began to **belt out** the school football fight song."

- "Without asking if I **minded,** he casually lit a cigar and then **tossed** the match onto my carpet—and couldn't understand why I was upset."

75
- "On the phone I had asked the candidate to bring his résumé and a couple of references. He arrived with the résumé—and two people."

Tom Kuntz

Copyright © 1999 by the New York Times Company. Reprinted by permission.

GLOSSARY

Fortune 1000 companies (n.) top 1000 nonfinancial corporations in the United States as ranked by sales by the business magazine *Fortune*

ill-conceived (adj.) badly formed or developed

management trainee position (n.) an entry-level position with potential for advancement to management

perk (n.) short for **perquisite** (n.) something received in addition to a regular wage or salary; a special benefit

sad sack (n.) a singularly awkward or clumsy person; a person lacking skill

QUICK COMPREHENSION CHECK

Complete the sentences with a word or phrase that fits in the blanks. Refer to the selection if you need to.

A good start to getting a job is to **(1)** _____, but the main goal is to **(2)** _____. The selection gives a number of examples of **(3)** _____. The examples came from a survey of **(4)** _____ **(5)** _____ at **(6)** _____ of the **(7)** _____ companies. The survey results are a **(8)** _____ of what not to do on a **(9)** _____.

QUESTIONS FOR THOUGHT AND DISCUSSION

1. According to the selection, what should a person do to prepare for a job interview?
2. Why is it a good idea to have a personal interview for a job?
3. What is the main goal of a job interview?
4. What happens when some people go on job interviews?
5. What is the source of the examples of behavior in the article?
6. Who conducted the survey?
7. Who paid for the survey?
8. How are the examples of behavior the same?

ANOTHER LOOK AT THE SELECTION

The following can be done in pairs or groups:

1. There are 20 examples of behavior. On a sheet of paper, number 1–20 and write a sentence about what is wrong with each behavior. Number 1 is done for you.

   • "The reason the candidate was taking so long to respond to a question became apparent when he began to snore."

   (1) The candidate fell asleep during the interview.

2. Do you agree that all of the examples are of wrong behavior? If you do not, where do you disagree? Why do you disagree?

3. In your opinion, were these examples in a first, second, or third interview for the job? Why?

4. How do you think the personnel executives reacted when the job applicants showed these behaviors?

VOCABULARY BUILDING

Exercise 1: Match the following words or expressions from Selection 2 with their meanings. They are in bold print in the selection to help you find them easily.

Vocabulary

_____ 1. belt out (v.)

_____ 2. boast [about] (v.)

_____ 3. crumple (v.)

_____ 4. get the word (v.)

_____ 5. mind (v.)

_____ 6. overalls (n.)

_____ 7. preach (v.)

_____ 8. primer (n.)

_____ 9. snore (v.)

_____ 10. stare [at] (v.)

_____ 11. take someone out of the running (v.)

_____ 12. toss (v.)

Meanings

a. to look steadily and directly

b. a book that covers the basic elements of a subject

c. loose-fitting pants with straps and a top part that covers the chest, worn as informal clothing

d. to throw something lightly or casually

e. to crush something so as to form creases or wrinkles

f. to sing something loudly

g. to teach and support something and urge others to follow

h. to be troubled or concerned about

i. to speak with too much pride about oneself; to brag

j. to remove someone from the competition for something

k. to understand the real importance of something

l. to breathe noisily through the nose and mouth while sleeping

Exercise 2: Complete the sentences with the correct vocabulary from Exercise 1. You may have to change the form of some of the words.

1. There are many books on the market that _____ about what to do during an interview for a job.

2. The list of behaviors in the selection "Next Time, Eat the Pizza after the Interview" is a _____ of what not to do on a job interview.

3. Self-defeating behavior can _____ for the position.

4. Some job candidates wore _____ and other inappropriate clothing.

5. Others _____ or _____ at the floor.

6. One candidate _____ her organizational skills and then gave a very poor example.

7. One person even _____ a school fight song.

8. Another candidate _____ the interviewer's business card and _____ it into the wastebasket.

9. The job candidates did not seem to care whether the interviewer _____ what they were doing.

10. They just did not _____.

Exercise 3: Answer the following in a few words or phrases:

1. What does "polish your shoes" mean? _____

2. What does "polish your résumé" mean? _____

3. What is a "self-help book"? Give an example of one. _____

4. What does "self-defeating behavior" mean? Give an example of such behavior. _____

IN YOUR WORDS

Write answers to the following:

1. With a partner, select one of the behaviors and write a short dialogue between the personnel executive and the job applicant. Practice your dialogue and role-play it to the rest of the class.

_____

_____

_____

2. Describe the correct behavior for a job interview.

_____

_____

_____

3. What advice would you give to a person going on a first interview for a job?

_____

_____

_____

SUMMING UP

1. As the class is role-playing the dialogues above, take notes on them. Then vote to choose which was the best.

2. Share your answer from number 2 above with the rest of the class. Then compose a class paragraph of what behavior should be during an interview.

3. Make a class list of advice for going on a first interview for a job.

4. Have the exercises for this selection answered the questions in your reading journal?

5. Remember to make your entries in your vocabulary log.

Selection 3

DISCOVER WHAT YOU THINK

1. Do you think that people should stay in the same jobs for their entire working lives? Why or why not?

_____

_____

_____

2. Do you think people in the United States stay in the same jobs for their entire careers? Why or why not?

_____

_____

_____

3. What about in your native land? Why or why not?

_____

_____

_____

4. Do you think that you will stay in the same job for your entire working life? Why or why not?

_____

_____

_____

_____

_____

HOW WE WORK NOW

TRAILBLAZERS: They're **freelancers** and **entrepreneurs,** low-key bosses and **border surfers** of the global marketplace. Some work for big corporations, some work only for No. 1. These **savvy, self-directed** folks are facing new challenges, forging their own paths—and reaping surprising rewards.

THE WORKER-IN-WAITING

Kristen ———, Lisle, Illinois

SKILL: She has the **smarts** not to choose her track too quickly. And she's figured out that college should be much more than four years of career training. PAYOFF: Resisting the current **mania** for careerism keeps all her options open. She'll be ready not just for a job when she gets out of school, but for a lifelong career.

For young people just starting to plan their careers, a hot job market can worsen the panic attacks. In today's money-nuts culture, the pressure to make perfect decisions is landing especially hard on high-school seniors applying to colleges. Many worry that a classic liberal-arts education will leave them **unemployable,** especially if the job market cools. High-schoolers **dump** these anxieties on teachers like Linda Brown of Benet Academy, a **topflight** Benedictine prep school outside Chicago. Armed with common sense and Kleenex, Brown helps students face their fears: Will there still be jobs? Will anybody want me?

Deciding what to make of college is difficult for Kristen ———, one of Benet's top seniors. Early on, she wanted to become a doctor. Now the prospects of teaching or doing biological research also **tug** at her heart. But several college application forms urged her to select a primary area of study before she's even admitted. "They ask you to check one box when you want to check five or six," says Kristen, 18, whose interests range from Latin Club to the tennis team. "I don't know what I want for a career. Is that wrong?"

Maybe it's smart. Some students make early career choices they come to **regret.** Brown sees a **backlash** with several of those who grew to **dislike** what they'd chosen now counseling younger students to take their time. "What you get from a liberal-arts education," Brown says, "is doors." Kristen is applying to schools like Georgetown, Princeton and Northwestern, where she can later migrate from an all-purpose curriculum to a professional track. In her view, she's educating herself for all the jobs she'll ever hold—not just the first.

John McCormick

From *Newsweek,* February 1, 1999. © 1999 by Newsweek, Inc. All rights reserved. Reprinted by permission.

THE RETREAD

David Evans, Warren, Michigan

SKILL: While others bellyache about retraining, he relishes technological change and learning. His **self-improvement** streak guarantees he'll never be **obsolete.**
PAYOFF: He's found a **niche** helping his peers adapt to the wired world and reminding younger workers that computer skills are only one **facet** of the job.

If you remove all the late-model cars from the parking lots, it's easy to imagine the **General Motors** Tech Center in the 1960s: populated by **crew-cut** engineers, the building filled with the smell of the clay used to mold car designs. David Evans remembers those days well. A 30-year **GM** veteran, he recalls how a dozen designers would hunch over a single **blueprint** in large, open studios. Today the Tech Center is a different place, cubicled, wired and aglow with computers. Like most companies, **GM** has entered the Information Age—and brought workers like Evans along for the ride.

For many of his **colleagues,** it's been an **arduous** journey. It's one thing to become **adept** at Microsoft Word; it's another to learn five different computer-aided design packages, as Evans has. Compounding the pressure: Evans, a "portfolio manager" who helps **GM** make sure **Buicks** don't look too much like **Oldsmobiles,** is 48 and working at a company that's wildly overstaffed. But Evans isn't sweating it. Like the classic cars **GM** was building when he signed on, he's been overhauled and **retuned.**

BACK TO SCHOOL. Technology-lover and avid learner Evans at his latest workstation

What sets Evans apart from others hit by big workplace changes is his enthusiasm for technology, his commitment to **self-improvement** and his healthy sense of perspective. On his 45-minute commute Evans listens to business audiotapes; at night he pursues a master's degree in system engineering,

75 even though he's 20 years older than most classmates. Each time **GM** upgrades its computers, he heads to training classes, knowing he'll be asking more questions than younger workers. He's **unfazed** because he understands the value he and other old-timers offer. "I have kids here who can really make a computer fly, but they don't have the years of experience making a car go down the road," Evans says. Today he's found a role helping **reluctant**

80 workers get accustomed to designing cars using **3-D** computer images—and reminding younger staffers to occasionally power down the computer and return to pen-and-paper drawing. Says Evans: I'm a technologist, but I think the best computers we have are the ones between our ears."

Daniel McGinn

From *Newsweek*, February 1, 1999. © 1999 by Newsweek, Inc. All rights reserved. Reprinted by permission.

THE CYBER PLUMBER

Joyce Huckaby, San Jose, California

85 SKILL: She can peer at the **innards** of high-tech contraptions to fix problems, and keeps studying to stay abreast of rapid technological change.
PAYOFF: The freedom of unsupervised work at **white-collar** wages, and job security in a world with more high-tech equipment than ever.

90 Five years ago Joyce Huckaby's life wasn't working out. A single mother with three children, she wound up on welfare,

95 in a shelter for the homeless, worried that the world was passing her by. Then Huckaby enrolled in the technical school at

100 Heald College, an 18-month program that **arms** students with the latest high-tech **expertise.** Today she has a home for her kids

105 and a $30,000-a-year job repairing the increasingly complex machines that are

NEW-COLLAR WORKER Huckaby fixing an emissions-testing machine at a dealership

used to diagnose and fix cars. "Shops pay $20,000 for a piece of equipment and don't open the manuals," she says. "That's job security."

110   Good jobs for folks who skip college are fading fast. As the economy changes, the best opportunities will be in technical niches like the one Huckaby has found opening the cabinets of today's high-tech equipment and—unlike the rest of us—making sense of what's inside. Think of these people as the **blue-collar** workers of the Information Age, who are thriving

115   in new jobs that provide a ticket to middle-class life. Huckaby's **alma mater,** the private, San Jose-based Heald, is one of about 1,000 such vocational schools around the county that offer technical degrees; in five years, enrollment in its $17,000, "applied science" program has doubled. Top graduates, who start the program with just a high-school diploma,

120   typically win job offers from companies like **Intel, IBM** or **Pacific Bell.**

Inspired by her parents, who run an automotive repair shop, Huckaby took a slightly different route: she fixes high-tech car-repair equipment like vehicle aligners, brake tuners and smog-testing machines. On a typical day she's at a Chrysler dealership on San Jose's sprawling Automall strip,

125   replacing a faulty circuit board in an emissions-testing unit. Later she's at a school, fixing equipment used to teach students in a shop class. Huckaby's office is her white company van, filled with brain-numbing guidebooks. "If I want to punish my children, I read them my operation manuals," she says. But it's no joke: half her job is keeping up with technological change.

130   Huckaby likes the fact that she's not tethered to a desk, gets her hands dirty (literally) and regularly solves problems that could **derail** many small businesses. "People **rely on** us for their well-being," she says. "We're the medics of metal."

Brad Stone

From *Newsweek,* February 1, 1999. © 1999 by Newsweek, Inc. All rights reserved. Reprinted by permission.

GLOSSARY

alma mater (n.) the school, college, or university that a person has attended

blue-collar (adj.) relating to wage earners whose jobs are performed in work clothes and often involve manual labor (*blue collar* originally referred to the blue shirt worn for manual labor)

blueprint (n.) a photographic copy of technical drawings appearing as white lines on a blue background

border surfer (n.) a person who works in different countries

Buick (n.) an automobile made by General Motors

crew-cut (adj.) a very short haircut

General Motors, **GM** (adj., n.) a large company that makes automobiles

innards (n.) the inner parts of a machine

Intel, IBM, Pacific Bell (n.) large companies that use high technology

Oldsmobile (n.) an automobile made by General Motors

savvy (adj.) well-informed; shrewd

smarts (n.) intelligence

3-D (adj.) three-dimensional

topflight (adj.) first-rate; excellent

trailblazer (n.) a leader in a field; a pioneer

white-collar (adj.) relating to professionals or workers whose work usually does not involve manual labor (*white-collar* originally referred to the white shirt worn for the office)

QUICK COMPREHENSION CHECK

There are three people discussed in the selection. Complete the following sentences with important information about each one. Refer to the selection if you need to.

1. Kristen —————— _____

_____

2. David Evans _____

_____

3. Joyce Huckaby _____

_____

Exercise 3: Fill in the blanks with the correct vocabulary from Exercise 2. You may have to change the form of some of the words.

1. Today in the United States there is a _____ for careerism.

2. There has been some _____ from students who chose their fields of study very early and later _____ the choice.

3. Because David Evans has kept up with the technological changes in his field, he has kept himself from becoming _____.

4. For some employees who have been in the workforce for awhile, adjusting to the computer age has been an _____ journey.

5. Employees who are _____ to use computers to design cars need special training.

6. David Evans assists _____ who need help designing cars using 3-D computer images.

7. Joyce Huckaby uses her _____ to fix complex machines that diagnose and repair cars.

8. Her customers _____ her to help them with their problems in their businesses.

9. There is room in United States for people who wish to be _____.

10. In addition, people who do not want to work for only one company can, in many cases, _____.

11. Today people have to explore and network to find their _____ in the work force.

5. What questions would you ask him or her?

_____

_____

_____

_____

SUMMING UP

1. Survey the class and find out which person the members would most like to meet. Why did they choose that person? Which people were ranked second and third?

2. Make a list of questions that the class would ask each of the three people.

3. Have the exercises for this selection helped you answer the questions in your reading journal?

4. Remember to make your entries in your vocabulary log.

REFLECTING AND SYNTHESIZING

A. Share your reading journal and vocabulary log with a partner or group. Discuss any questions or observations that you have. Is your vocabulary log helping you build your vocabulary? Why or why not?

B. After answering the following, share your thoughts with your partner, group, or class:

1. What advice would you give to someone who wants to attend a college or university in the United States?

2. Compare the work world here with the work world where you came from. What is the same? What is different?

3. Which do you prefer, the work world here or where you came from? Why?

4. How have each of the people in Selection 3 "hitched their wagons to stars"?

5. What are the advantages and disadvantages of having your own business?

C. Answer these questions on your own:

1. How are you "hitching your wagon to a star"?

2. Write about one of the happiest times you had during your college or university experience.

3. Write about one of the worst times you had during your college or university experience.

4. Write about one of your own experiences on a job interview.

5. Describe your "dream" job, the perfect job for you.

6. If you could have your own business, describe what kind you would have.

7. Did your ideas about education or employment change as a result of the material in this chapter? If yes, how? If not, why not? What did you think before you read the chapter and what do you think now?

4

LOOKING FORWARD: BEING A WISE CONSUMER IN THE UNITED STATES

OPENING THOUGHT

Caveat emptor **(Latin)—Let the buyer beware.**

Take a few minutes to think about the words that introduce this chapter. Answer the following questions:

1. What do you think the words mean?

_____

_____

_____

_____

_____

2. Do you agree or disagree with them? Why?

_____

_____

_____

_____

_____

3. Can you think of a situation where you as a buyer should have taken the advice of these words?

_____

_____

_____

_____

Share your thoughts with your partner, group, or class.

Selection 1

DISCOVER WHAT YOU KNOW AND THINK

1. What is the biggest shopping season in the United States?

_____

2. Do you think that people should have charge cards from individual stores and/or credit cards? Why or why not?

_____

_____

_____

_____

3. Do you think that it is easy or difficult to get into financial problems in the United States? Why or why not?

_____

_____

_____

_____

4. When purchasing a large item, such as a car or computer, how do you decide which brand or kind to buy?

_____

_____

_____

_____

WHEN SHOPPING FOR HOLIDAYS, 'BUYER BEWARE' IS STILL BEST ADVICE

With the holiday shopping **barrage** about to descend upon us, the old-time **adage** of "buyer beware" may yet be the best advice for shoppers bombarded with a bewildering **array** of product choices and advertising **blitzes.**

. . .

"Staying on budget and resisting the urge to buy impulsively is one of the best gifts you can give your loved ones this holiday season," says Rob Schneider, a senior policy analyst with the Southwest Regional Office of Consumers Union. "By planning ahead, you can ensure you're not saddled with additional unplanned debt when the party's over."

To help with the busiest shopping days of the year, Consumers Union offers the following tips:

Be careful with how you pay

- Set aside what you can afford to spend on gifts and stick to the plan. *Paying with cash* can help you stay on budget. But it has drawbacks, too, including concerns about security and the possibility you may encounter difficulty when returning **defective** merchandise.

- *Credit cards* can be a useful tool, particularly for items that have to be delivered or that might break down. But be **wary** of store credit cards—they usually carry high interest rates and are designed to keep you coming back for more purchases. Also don't take cash advances on a credit card. Cash advances cost even more than credit card purchases since you also pay a fee of 2 percent or more of the amount of the advance. Also, cash advances usually carry no **grace periods.**

- If you use a *debit card,* understand the risks. A debit card takes money right out of your checking account, and if lost or stolen, it is possible your account could be drained. It's more like paying with cash than either a check or a credit card. Plus, you can't stop payment or have the right to **dispute** payment if the goods are defective. If theft occurs, Visa and Mastercard have promised to voluntarily recredit accounts, but it may not be worth the **hassles.**

- Another tempting Christmas shopping offer is *deferred payment plans* ("No payments for six months!") Unless you can pay off the full balance by the due date, don't fall for this trap. Companies plan to

35 make big profits on their finance charges, which may start from the original dates of purchase.

- Be careful using a ***home equity loan*** to pay holiday bills or credit card debts. Home equity loans should be used for specific, planned expenditures, such as tuition or home improvements. Taking a home **40** equity loan to **consolidate** your debts could worsen your financial problems. If you can't pay back the loan, you could lose your house.

Extended warranties usually are a poor buy

Stores often push **extended warranties** on their products, but these are usually not a good deal for consumers. Fewer than 20 percent of products **45** covered by an extended warranty are ever brought in for repair. According to a May 1998 Consumer Reports survey, readers who bought extended warranties had paid about as much for those warranties as the average repair costs for each item. Instead, pay the extra money for a high quality product or set aside a repair fund. Sometimes credit cards automatically include **50** extended warranties, but be sure you read the fine print. However, you may want to consider an extended warranty for certain high tech products subject to frequent use like home computers.

Which is the best way to pay for purchases?
Cash, credit card, debit card, deferred payment plan, home equity loan?

Shopping on-line is not for everyone

55

60

Purchasing products from catalogs or over the Internet has many advantages: it cuts off time spent traveling from store to store, business hours are more flexible for even 24 hours a day, and many businesses have a better selection of items compared to your local mall. If you are new to on-line shopping, it is wise to start with a small purchase such as a book or CD. Also, shop with someone you know and trust and make sure the seller has a good privacy policy.

If security remains a concern, you can still comparison shop on-line and then make your purchase in person.

Know the return policy before buying

65

70

Always save your receipts or other proof of purchase, and ask the retailers what their return policy is before you buy. If the product doesn't work as advertised, promptly take it back and ask for a refund or replacement. If you are still dissatisfied, contact the seller or manufacturer in writing. Be polite but persistent in pursuing your complaint. If you are not satisfied, complain in writing to the Texas Attorney General's office. [Or to the Attorney General's or consumer advocate's office in the state where you live.]

Consider alternatives to buying

75

In response to the shopping craze that occurs every year, on the day after Thanksgiving a Buy Nothing Day has been started to encourage people to stop and reflect on the holiday excesses. Instead of shopping, you can plan to spend the day with family and anticipate any groceries or other needs ahead of time. Also, as the malls get more and more crowded, consider alternative gifts. For example, a charitable contribution made in the recipient's name can be an ideal gift that **exemplifies** the true spirit of the holiday season. And don't forget too that sometimes the best gifts are homemade ones.

80

Seek help if debt becomes a problem

If you have trouble with your debts, contact the nonprofit Consumer Credit Counseling Service in your area to help you budget and to negotiate a payment plan with your creditors. Call 1-800-777-7526 (777-PLAN) for a local listing.

85

Said CU's Schneider: "Shoppers are particularly vulnerable during the holiday season and merchants know it. It all **boils down** to common sense. It is up to each consumer to be informed and protect their hard earned money."

"When Shopping for the Holidays, 'Buyer Beware' is Still Best Advice," as reprinted from http://www.consumersunion.org. Copyright © 1998 Consumers Union. Reprinted by permission.

GLOSSARY

adage (n.) a short proverb or saying generally considered to be wise or true

array (n.) an impressively large number

barrage (n.) an overwhelming outpouring

blitz (n.) an intense effort or campaign

boil down (v.) to reduce to a simpler form

consolidate (v.) to combine (two or more items) into one

defective (adj.) having a defect or flaw; faulty

dispute (v.) to debate or argue about something

exemplify (v.) to be an example of something; illustrate

extended warranty (n.) an agreement to increase or extend the period of guarantee beyond the manufacturer's original guarantee period

grace period (n.) a period in which a debt may be paid without accruing interest or penalty

hassle (n.) trouble or bother

home equity loan (n.) usually a second mortgage reflecting the owner's unmortgaged value of the home

wary (adj.) on guard; watchful

QUICK COMPREHENSION CHECK

Complete the sentences with a word or phrase that fits in the blanks. Refer to the selection if you need to.

Rob Schneider of **(1)** _____ says that shoppers should stay on **(2)** _____ and not buy **(3)** _____ during the holiday shopping season. To help with shopping, several tips are offered. First, be careful **(4)** _____. Different ways of paying are discussed including **(5)** _____,

(6) _____, **(7)** _____,
(8) _____, and **(9)** _____.
Second, extended warranties are not a **(10)** _____.
Third, shopping on the Internet has **(11)** _____
but is not **(12)** _____. Fourth, a consumer must
know the **(13)** _____ before purchasing
something. And finally, alternatives to buying are suggested including
(14) _____, **(15)** _____,
and **(16)** _____. If consumers have problems
with debts, they can **(17)** _____.

QUESTIONS FOR THOUGHT AND DISCUSSION

1. What advice does Rob Schneider of Consumers Union give to shoppers?

2. What are the advantages and disadvantages of paying with cash?

3. What is the difference between a credit card and a debit card?

4. Should a person take a cash advance on a credit card? Why or why not?

5. When should a shopper take advantage of a deferred payment plan?

6. Should a shopper use a home equity loan to pay off bills or credit card debts? Why or why not?

7. Should a shopper purchase an extended warranty on a purchase? Why or why not?

8. What advice does the selection give for on-line shopping?

9. If a purchase is defective, what should a consumer do?

10. What do you think of the suggestion of a Buy Nothing Day?

11. What other alternatives to purchasing does the selection suggest? Can you think of any additional alternatives?

12. If consumers have trouble with debt, what can they do?

ANOTHER LOOK AT THE SELECTION

You can do the following exercises in pairs or groups:

Part I. Read the following situations and, using the information in the selection, answer the questions:

A. Elana is a full-time student who also works part-time in the library on campus. She is on scholarship and has to maintain a B average. She wants to buy a compact disk (CD) player as well as at least 25 disks of her favorite music. She found an offer where she can purchase the player and not have to make any payments for six months.

   1. What questions should she ask about the offer?

   2. What do you think she should do? Why?

B. Marco, a college student, has two credit cards and he has used the credit on both cards to the maximum. In other words, he has "maxed out" his cards. He works 40 hours a week at a gas station. He can only afford to make the minimum payments on the cards.

   1. What choices does he have?

   2. Which do you recommend and why?

C. Hiroko purchased a video tape player from a large chain store. However, it does not work properly. She took it back to the store with her receipt for its purchase. The clerk tested it and said that it was fine. She took it home again, but it still doesn't work properly.

   1. What choices does she have?

   2. Which do you recommend and why?

D. Alex, a full-time commuting student, decided to buy a computer for use at home. The salesperson is pressuring him to buy an extended warranty on the machine. Alex has talked to some of his friends who said that he should not purchase the warranty.

   1. What should he do?

   2. Why?

E. Create a situation of your own based on information in the selection and share it with a partner.

F. With a partner choose one of the situations and write a short dialogue based on it. Then perform it for the class.

Part II. The following reading gives more information about Consumers Union. Read it and answer the True/False questions that follow.

ABOUT CONSUMERS UNION

CONSUMERS UNION, publisher of *Consumer Reports,* is an independent, nonprofit testing and consumer-protection organization serving only consumers. Since 1936, it has been a comprehensive source for unbiased reporting about products and services, personal finance, health and nutrition, and other consumer concerns.

Staff buy what they test off the shelf; they accept no free samples.

They test products in 50 state-of-the-art labs at their National Testing and Research Center in Yonkers, N. Y. Ratings are based on lab tests, controlled-use tests, and expert judgments by the technical and research staff. If a product is high in overall quality and relatively low in price, they deem it a CR Best Buy. A rating refers only to the brand and model listed.

They survey millions of readers to report on the reliability of hundreds of auto models, and of products such as appliances and electronic gear. Reader-survey data also help them to report on other consumer services.

They accept no ads from companies, and they don't let any company use their reports or Ratings for commercial purposes. They do advertise their own services, which provide impartial information to consumers.

Their three advocacy offices and Consumer Policy Institute address the crucial task of influencing policy that affects consumers, which is so integral to Consumer Union's mission.

Consumers Union's advocates tackle consumer issues that are regional, national, and even international in scope from their offices in Washington, D.C.; San Francisco, California; and Austin, Texas. They testify before Federal and state legislative and regulatory bodies, petition government agencies, and file lawsuits on behalf of the consumer interest.

The Consumer Policy Institute, at Consumers Union's headquarters in Yonkers, New York, promotes the consumer interest through research and education projects—conferences, policy papers, and comment on legislative and regulatory initiatives.

Consumer Reports, June 1999, Consumers Union, p. 6 and Web site About Consumers Union
    http://www.consumersunion.org/aboutcu/about.htm

QUICK COMPREHENSION CHECK ☑

Write *T* for true or *F* for false. Refer to the selection if you need to.

_____ **1.** Consumers Union, a consumer-protection organization, is run for profit.

_____ **2.** It publishes a magazine called *Consumer Reports.*

_____ **3.** Consumers Union is based in Yonkers, New York.

_____ **4.** It has contracts with outside laboratories that test products, which are then given ratings.

_____ **5.** Companies are permitted to use Consumers Union reports for their own commercial purposes.

_____ **6.** Consumers Union works only on national consumer issues.

VOCABULARY BUILDING

> **VOCABULARY STRATEGY:**
> Learning some of the common prefixes, syllables placed at the beginning of a word to change its meaning, can help you to build your vocabulary. Likewise, learning some of the common suffixes, syllables placed at the ends of words, can also help you to build your vocabulary. Following is a list of common suffixes and their meanings with some vocabulary examples. Use suffixes to help you figure out the meanings of words. Enter the suffixes that are new to you or that you are not sure of in your **vocabulary log.**

SUFFIX	MEANING	SAMPLE WORDS
-able	Forms adjectives that mean "capable or worthy of"	breakable, honorable, likeable, washable
-ible	Has the same meaning as **-able**	credible, flexible
-al sometimes **–ial**	Relating to or characterized by	adjectival, postal commercial
-ate	Characterized by Rank; office To act upon in a specified manner	fortunate consulate insulate, stimulate
-ation	Added to a verb and changes that verb to a noun	create-creation civilize-civilization starve-starvation
-ative	Means of, relating to, or associated with	talkative, authoritative
-en	To cause to be or to become. When added to nouns and adjectives, **-en** forms verbs. Made of; resembling. Changes nouns into adjectives	cheapen, redden, soften threaten, widen wooden, golden
-er	Person or thing that does a specified action A person who is born or lives in a place A person or thing that is associated or involved with	swimmer, blender, dryer, washer islander, New Yorker foreigner, six-footer, banker, gardener
-ess	Female	heiress, lioness
-ette	Small Female Imitation or substitute	kitchenette majorette leatherette
-ful	Means "full." Added to nouns to make adjectives meaning "full of" or "having" the quality shown by the noun When added to a noun to form another noun, means "a quantity that would fill" a container	careful, playful cupful, mouthful
-fy	Verb suffix that means "to make or cause something to become"; **-fy** normally takes the form **-ify**	acidify, humidify, purify

SUFFIX	MEANING	SAMPLE WORDS
-ic	Relating to or characterized by	allergic, atomic
-ism	Forms nouns. Means "the act, state, or theory of"	pacifism
-ist	Forms nouns that denote somebody who does something	biologist, conformist, cyclist, specialist
-ize	Turns nouns and adjectives into verbs	formalize, jeopardize, hospitalize, legalize
-less	Without, lacking Not able to act in a certain way	careless, fearless, headless, loveless relentless
-like	Similar to or characteristic of	childlike, lifelike
-ly	Having the characteristics of Recurring at a specific interval of time In a specified manner At a specified interval	sisterly hourly gradually weekly, yearly
-ment	Forms nouns	amazement, entertainment, government
-ness	Forms nouns that mean "state," "condition," or "quality"	brightness, cleanliness, neighborliness, willingness
-oid	Like or resembling	humanoid, spheroid
-or	Person or thing that performs State, quality, or activity	competitor, accelerator valor, honor
-ous	Forms adjectives meaning having, full of, or characterized by	adventurous, humorous, joyous
-ship	Particular state or condition Qualities belong to a class of human beings Rank or office	friendship, hardship, relationship craftsmanship, sportsmanship ambassadorship
-ward **-wards**	Having a particular direction or location; forms adjectives and adverbs Adverbs ending in **-ward** can also end in **-wards**	backward, forward, upward, homeward I stepped backward. I stepped backwards.

Exercise 1: Use the vocabulary in the following list to fill in the blanks in the sentences. Use the sentence context to help choose the correct word. You may have to change the form of some of the words.

authoritative	joyous	redden
competitor	lifelike	six-footer
hardship	postal	upward
insulate	purify	willingness

1. He was a _____, so he thought he would have a good chance to get on the basketball team.

2. The refugees from the war suffered many _____ on their way to safety.

3. Frequently at dawn the sky _____ as the sun comes up.

4. The whole family came together to celebrate the _____ occasion.

5. People who work in the business world are sometimes very fierce

   _____.

6. Jobs in the United States _____ Service have very good benefits.

7. The silk flowers were so beautifully made that they looked

   _____.

8. My brother expressed _____ to lend me the money when I told him I wanted it for tuition.

9. Since the winters were very cold, the couple decided to _____ their house better.

10. When Angela looked _____, she saw that the night sky was filled with stars.

11. The policeman who stopped us on the highway acted in a very

    _____ manner.

12. You can use chlorine to _____ water for drinking.

Exercise 2: In Selection 1, find words with the given suffixes. Write the words in the blanks.

1. Find one adjective with the suffix *-al.*

   _____

2. Find four nouns with the suffix *-er.*

   _____

3. Find one verb with the suffix *-fy* or *-fies.*

   _____

4. Find one adjective with the suffix *-able* and one with *-ible.*

   _____

5. Find three adverbs with the suffix *-ly.*

   _____

6. Find two nouns with the suffix *-ment.*

   _____

IN YOUR WORDS

Write a few sentences to answer each of the following:

1. This selection was written for the end-of-year holiday shopping in the United States. Do you think that the advice in it can be used for any shopping throughout the year? Why or why not?

   _____

   _____

2. Has reading the material in this selection changed your thinking about being a consumer in the United States? How?

   _____

   _____

3. In your opinion, what is the biggest temptation about shopping in the United States?

   _____

   _____

SUMMING UP

1. Share your answers to numbers 1, 2, and 3 from In Your Words.

2. Choose one of the three and write a summary paragraph of the group or class responses.

3. Remember your reading journal and your vocabulary log.

Selection 2

DISCOVER WHAT YOU THINK

1. Must a person have a lot of money to lead a happy life? Why or why not?

_____

_____

_____

_____

2. What do you think provides for happiness in life?

_____

_____

_____

_____

3. Do you think people place more emphasis on money in the United States than they do in other cultures? Why or why not?

_____

_____

_____

_____

IN PURSUIT OF AFFLUENCE, AT A HIGH PRICE

The adage that money cannot buy happiness may be familiar, but is easily forgotten in a consumer society. A much more persistent and seductive message is beamed from every television screen: Contentment is available for the price of this car, that computer, a little more getting and spending.

Over the last few years, however, psychological researchers have been **amassing** an impressive body of data suggesting that satisfaction simply is not for sale. Not only does having more things prove to be unfulfilling, but people for whom **affluence** is a **priority** in life tend to experience an unusual degree of anxiety and depression as well as a lower overall level of well-being. Likewise, those who would like nothing more than to be famous or attractive do not fare as well, psychologically speaking, as those who primarily want to develop close relationships, become more self-aware, or contribute to the community.

Earlier research had demonstrated that neither income nor attractiveness was strongly correlated with a sense of well-being. But Dr. Richard Ryan, professor of psychology at the University of Rochester, and Dr. Tim Kasser, a former student who is now an assistant professor of psychology at Knox College in Illinois, have discovered that the news is even worse.

In three sets of studies published in leading psychology journals since 1993, with a new article expected later this year in Personality and Social Psychology Bulletin and still more papers on the way, the researchers sketch an increasingly **bleak** portrait of people who value "**extrinsic** goals" like money, fame and beauty.

Such people are not only more depressed than others, but also report more

behavioral problems and physical discomfort, as well as scoring lower on
40 measures of **vitality** and **self-actualization.** While not every study has
investigated the full list of effects, the pattern that emerges from the research
project as a whole is remarkably **consistent.**

Dr. Ryan and Dr. Kasser said their studies provided a look at the "dark
side of the American dream," noting that the culture in some ways seemed to
45 be built on precisely what turned out to be **detrimental** to mental health.
Americans are encouraged to try to strike it rich, but "the more we seek
satisfactions in material goods, the less we find them there," Dr. Ryan said.
"The satisfaction has a short half-life; it's very **fleeting.**"

Moreover, the detrimental effect of extrinsic goals seems to hold
50 regardless of age or even level of income: A preoccupation with money
bodes ill regardless of how much money one already has. The effects also
appear not to be limited to any one culture. Dr. Kasser and his associates
have now collected data from subjects in 13 countries, including Germany,
Russia and India. The fact that pursuing wealth is psychologically unhelpful
55 and often destructive, he reports, "comes through very strongly in every
culture I've looked at."

. . .

Another study by the same researchers, not yet accepted for publication,
found that college students who were already "relatively high in the
attainment of appearance, financial success and popularity" were
60 nevertheless "lower in well-being and self-esteem." Those who **aspired** to
affluence also had more **transient** relationships, watched more television
and were more likely to use cigarettes, alcohol and other drugs than were
those who placed less emphasis on extrinsic goals.

Apart from its obvious implications for a culture that **thrives** on material
65 gain, this whole line of research raises questions about the **proclivity** of
some psychologists to analyze the dynamics of what is often called goal-
directed behavior while, in effect, ignoring the nature of the goal. Likewise,
it challenges **homespun** advice to "follow one's dream," whatever it may be.

These data strongly suggest that not all goals or dreams are created equal.
70 According to the researchers, pursuing goals that reflect genuine human
needs, like wanting to feel connected to others, turns out to be more
psychologically beneficial than spending one's life trying to impress others
or to **accumulate** trendy clothes, fancy **gizmos** and the money to keep
buying them.

. . .

GLOSSARY

accumulate (n.) to collect or gather something together

affluence (n.) wealth

amass (v.) to gather something

aspire (v.) desire strongly

bleak (adj.) gloomy; dreary; depressing

bode ill (v.) to be a bad sign

consistent (adj.) continually following the same principles

detrimental (adj.) causing damage or harm

extrinsic (adj.) originating from the outside; external

fleeting (adj.) passing quickly; very brief

gizmo (n.) a small device whose name is forgotten or not yet known

homespun (adj.) plain and simple

priority (n.) something considered in terms of its importance relative to other matters

proclivity (n.) natural inclination

self-actualization (n.) realizing the potential of the self

thrive (v.) to grow in a healthy way; flourish

transient (adj.) lasting only a short time

vitality (n.) physical or mental vigor; energy

QUICK COMPREHENSION CHECK

Complete the sentences with a word or phrase that fits in the blanks. Refer to the selection if you need to.

In a consumer society the message is that **(1)** _____

can buy **(2)** _____. However, psychological researchers

have been gathering data that suggest this is **(3)** _____.

Recent studies have shown that the picture is even **(4)** _____

for people who value "extrinsic goals" like **(5)** _____,

(6) _____, and **(7)** _____.

Such people **(8)** _____. American culture seems to be

built on what is **(9)** _____ to mental health.

This negative effect of extrinsic goals seems to be true regardless of

(10) _____, **(11)** _____

or **(12)** _____. College students who aspired to wealth

(13) _____. Finally, according to the researchers,

pursuing goals that **(14)** _____ is better than trying to

(15) _____ or to **(16)** _____.

QUESTIONS FOR THOUGHT AND DISCUSSION

1. What is the message that surrounds those who live in a consumer society?

2. What do the data that psychological researchers have gathered suggest about money and contentment?

3. What about people who want nothing more than to be famous or attractive?

4. What have Drs. Ryan and Kasser discovered through their research?

5. Define *extrinsic goals.*

6. What does American culture encourage regarding material goods?

7. What about age, level of income, and other cultures and the pursuit of wealth?

8. Where is the problem with affluence?

9. What picture of college students do the researchers present in another study?

10. What do some psychologists tend to do in their research on goal-directed behavior?

11. According to the researchers, what is psychologically beneficial for people?

12. What is not psychologically beneficial?

ANOTHER LOOK AT THE SELECTION

You can do the following exercises in pairs or groups:

1. The following is a quote from the selection:

> Dr. Kasser and his associates have now collected data from subjects in 13 countries, including Germany, Russia and India. The fact that pursuing wealth is psychologically unhelpful and often destructive, he reports, "comes through very strongly in every culture I've looked at."

Do you agree with Dr. Kasser and his associates? What questions would you like to ask Dr. Kasser about the quote above? Do you think that the statement is true in the culture from which you came? Why or why not?

2. Read the paragraph following the quote in number 1, starting on line 58. Do you agree with the researchers? What questions would you like to ask the researchers about the paragraph? Do you think that the statement is true based on your observation of college or university students? Why or why not?

3. The selection states, "These data strongly suggest that not all goals or dreams are created equal." Do you agree or disagree with this statement? Why?

VOCABULARY BUILDING

Exercise 1: Find words with the given prefixes or suffixes in Selection 2.

1. Find three adjectives that use the prefix *un-*.

_____

2. Find three adjectives that have the suffix *–al.*

_____

3. Find three words that have the prefix *self-*.

_____

4. Find one word with the suffix *–er* that means "the person who does a specified action."

_____

5. Find two nouns with the suffix *–ment.*

_____

6. Find one noun with the suffix *–ness.*

_____

> **VOCABULARY STRATEGY:**
> Determining the job of the word in a sentence can also help you be a better reader. Knowing if the word is a noun, pronoun, verb, adjective, adverb, preposition, or conjunction may help you to understand it. Following are the definitions of these terms.

1. **Noun:** a word that is used to name a person, a place, a thing, a quality, or an action and that functions as the subject or object of a verb or as the object of a preposition.

   In the sentence

   > The man sent the box by mail.

   the words *man, box,* and *mail* are nouns.

2. **Pronoun:** any of a class of words used as substitutes for nouns or noun phrases.

   > Maria is *my* friend. *She* is in my English class.
   > Joe lost *his* wallet. *He* thinks that *he* lost *it* in the mall.

   In the sentences above, the italicized words are all pronouns. *She, He, he,* and *it* are pronouns. *My* and *his* are possessive adjectives that have a pronoun function.

3. **Verb:** a word, such as *be, run,* or *happen,* that shows existence, action, or occurrence. Or a phrase, such as *has been thinking,* that is a verb form.

4. **Adjective:** a word used to modify a noun by describing it, limiting it, or adding to its meaning.

   > The *young* boy is very *tall*.

   The adjectives are *young* and *tall*.

   In English, adjectives usually appear before the noun they modify, but with verbs such as *act, seem,* and *be,* they often appear after the verb as in

   > The mouse acts *nervous.*
   > The cat seems *happy.*
   > The horse is *thirsty.*

5. **Adverb:** a word used to describe or add meaning to a verb, an adjective, or another adverb.

   > They left *early.*
   > The peacock is *very* pretty.
   > The dog ran *very fast.*

   The adverbs are *early, very,* and *fast.*

6. **Preposition:** a word placed before a noun or pronoun that shows the relationship, such as location, time, or direction, between that noun or pronoun and another word. *To, at,* and *in* are common prepositions.

> The mother saw him walking *to* school.
> I'll pick you up *at* three o'clock.
> Tomás saw the thunderstorm *in* the west.

7. **Conjunction:** a word, such as *and, but, or,* or *yet,* that connects other words in a sentence.

> My son loves peanut butter *and* jelly sandwiches.
> Ellen was sick, *but* she went to work.
> Dad is either in the garage *or* on the porch.
> He loved her, *yet* he knew he had to leave her.

Exercise 2: Use the vocabulary in the following list to complete the sentences. Use your knowledge of nouns, adjectives, adverbs, and verbs to help you do the exercise. You may have to change the form of some words.

blender	craftsmanship	humidify	mouthful
cheapen	homeward	kitchenette	neighborliness
conformist	humanoid	loveless	sisterly

1. After traveling for six weeks, Magda's thoughts began to turn _____.

2. The mother insisted that the child at least try a _____ of each kind of food on the plate.

3. The problem with the apartment that I was looking at was that it only had a _____ and I love to cook.

4. As José loves milkshakes, he decided to buy himself a _____.

5. The house is very dry in the winter, so we are going to do something to _____ it.

6. Nina is a good friend, who acts very _____ towards me.

7. The handmade wooden boat was beautiful and showed a high degree of _____.

8. There are many different types of robots in factories today, but, unlike science fiction, few of them have _____ characteristics.

9. Allen decided that his marriage was _____, so he called a lawyer to find out about a no-fault divorce.

10. When the newly married couple moved into their new apartment, they were very surprised by the _____ of the tenants on their floor, who left them presents at their door.

11. She follows the current styles in her dress; indeed, she is a _____ when it comes to fashion.

12. Pirated video tapes _____ the value of those that are genuine.

IN YOUR WORDS

Write a few sentences to answer the following:

1. What questions would you like to ask the researchers?

_____

_____

2. Do you think that it is easy or difficult to live in a consumer society like the United States? Why or why not?

_____

_____

3. What advice about money would you give to someone who is coming to live in the United States?

_____

_____

_____

SUMMING UP

1. Share your answers to the three questions in In Your Words.

2. Make a list of the questions class members would like to ask the researchers.

3. Write a summary of the class responses to either question 1 or 2.

4. Remember your reading journal and vocabulary log.

Selection 3

DISCOVER WHAT YOU THINK

1. Do you think that it is a good idea to use the Internet to find information? Why or why not?

_____

_____

_____

2. Do you think that it is a good idea to shop on line? Why or why not?

_____

_____

3. What advice would you give to someone who is using the Internet?

_____

_____

WHALES IN THE MINNESOTA RIVER?

Only on the Web, Where Skepticism Is a Required Navigational Aid

Tourists drove six hours to Mankato, Minnesota, in search of underground caves and hot springs mentioned on a Web site. When they arrived, there were no such attractions.

. . .

5 And **bibliophiles** who trust the **grande dame** of on-line retailers, Amazon.com, for suggestions under the headings of "Destined for Greatness" and "What We're Reading" were **dismayed** to learn that some publishers had paid for special treatment for their books—meaning a more accurate heading would have been "What We're Paid to Say We're Reading."

10 (After the disclosure, Amazon added a note on its home page to make a **subtle** acknowledgement of the practice.)

On the World Wide Web, straight facts can be hard to find. After plowing through dense and **recalcitrant** search engines that offer more sites than you

payola (n.) bribe

pixel (n.) the smallest unit on a computer or television screen that with many others creates an electronic image

prey (n.) victim

recalcitrant (adj.) not willing to do what somebody who has power tells it to do

sales pitch (n.) a line of talk designed to persuade

skepticism (n.) a doubting or questioning attitude or state of mind

spoof (n.) an imitation of something that makes fun of it

subtle (n.) not immediately obvious

ticked (adj.) angry

toggle (v.) to give off a signal

triangulate (v.) to verify by using at least two more sources or points

QUICK COMPREHENSION CHECK

Complete the sentences with a word or phrase that fits in the blanks. Refer to the selection if you need to.

On the World Wide Web **(1)** _____ can be hard to find. The Web is largely **(2)** _____, so experts say that users must be **(3)** _____. They must ask questions. Who was **(4)** _____? Is the information **(5)** _____, **(6)** _____, and **(7)** _____? Can it be **(8)** _____ or the source **(9)** _____? Don Ray has the **(10)** _____ test to apply to Web research. This test makes users **(11)** _____. People who are going to spend money based on information from the Web should be very **(12)** _____. Paul Gilster says that Web users have to be their own **(13)** _____. Finally, Tara Calishain says that to check citations, a **(14)** _____ is the user's best friend.

QUESTIONS FOR THOUGHT AND DISCUSSION

1. There are two examples from the Web in which information given was not completely accurate. What are they?

2. Where is Minnesota? What is the climate there in winter?

3. Why is getting accurate, reliable information on the Web a problem?

4. In order to get accurate, reliable information on the Web, what does the user have to do?

5. There are three people mentioned in the selection. On the following lines, summarize what they are saying in one sentence:

Don Ray _____

_____

_____

Paul Gilster _____

_____

_____

Tara Calishain _____

_____

_____

ANOTHER LOOK AT THE SELECTION

You can do he following exercises in pairs or groups:

1. Read paragraphs one and two of the selection again. What is the author using to introduce the reader to the article?

2. Can you think of an example from your own experience using the Web that you could add to the introduction? Write a paragraph about your example.

3. In the selection Don Ray says that if a Web page has grammatical errors, sloppy spelling, or a goofy design, that makes him distrust the content. Do you agree with this judgment? Why or why not?

VOCABULARY BUILDING

Exercise 1: This selection contains many words associated with computers. These words are part of special computer vocabulary. Use the vocabulary strategies that you have read in this book to try to figure out the meanings of the words in bold print below. If you cannot figure them out, you will have to look in a dictionary. It will have to be a dictionary that has been published recently as these words entered English vocabulary with the widespread use of computers.

1. After the disclosure, Amazon added a note on its **home page** to make a subtle acknowledgement of the practice.

   home page ⸺⸺⸺⸺⸺⸺⸺⸺⸺⸺⸺⸺⸺

2. On the **World Wide Web**, straight facts can be hard to find.

   World Wide Web ⸺⸺⸺⸺⸺⸺⸺⸺⸺⸺⸺

3. After plowing through dense and recalcitrant **search engines** that offer more **sites** than you can point a **mouse** at, after enduring delays, lost **links,** and dead ends and arriving at a **site** that looks just right, **Web surfers** must deal with uncertainty . . .

   a. search engines ⸺⸺⸺⸺⸺⸺⸺⸺⸺⸺

   ⸺⸺⸺⸺⸺⸺⸺⸺⸺⸺⸺⸺⸺⸺⸺⸺

   b. site ⸺⸺⸺⸺⸺⸺⸺⸺⸺⸺⸺⸺⸺⸺

   ⸺⸺⸺⸺⸺⸺⸺⸺⸺⸺⸺⸺⸺⸺⸺⸺

   c. mouse ⸺⸺⸺⸺⸺⸺⸺⸺⸺⸺⸺⸺⸺

   ⸺⸺⸺⸺⸺⸺⸺⸺⸺⸺⸺⸺⸺⸺⸺⸺

   d. link ⸺⸺⸺⸺⸺⸺⸺⸺⸺⸺⸺⸺⸺⸺

   ⸺⸺⸺⸺⸺⸺⸺⸺⸺⸺⸺⸺⸺⸺⸺⸺

   e. Web surfer ⸺⸺⸺⸺⸺⸺⸺⸺⸺⸺⸺⸺

   ⸺⸺⸺⸺⸺⸺⸺⸺⸺⸺⸺⸺⸺⸺⸺⸺

4. Add three words below from your own computer vocabulary.

   ⸺⸺⸺⸺⸺⸺⸺⸺⸺⸺⸺⸺⸺⸺⸺⸺

   ⸺⸺⸺⸺⸺⸺⸺⸺⸺⸺⸺⸺⸺⸺⸺⸺

   ⸺⸺⸺⸺⸺⸺⸺⸺⸺⸺⸺⸺⸺⸺⸺⸺

Exercise 2: A **homonym** is a word that has the same sound and sometimes the same spelling as another word but a different meaning and origin.

1. In the following passage from the selection, there are two homonyms. What are they? What do they mean? What is the problem with their usage?

   > "Mankato, as portrayed on these pages, DOES NOT EXIST! PLEASE, do not come here to see these sites." Er, sights. (Of course, anybody looking at a map would probably be suspicious about the site's statement that "the winter temperature in many Mankato neighborhoods has never dropped below a balmy 70 degrees!")

   a. First homonym: _____

   　　Meaning: _____

   b. second Homonym: _____

   　　Meaning: _____

   c. Why did the author of the selection, Tina Kelley, write "Er, sights"?

   _____

2. *Red* and *read* are homonyms. Write two sentences showing the meanings of these words.

   _____

   _____

   _____

   _____

3. *Great* and *grate* are homonyms. Write two sentences showing the meanings of these words.

   _____

   _____

   _____

   _____

4. *Here* and *hear* are homonyms. Write two sentences showing the meanings of these words.

_____

_____

_____

_____

5. *Be* and *bee* are homonyms. Write two sentences showing the meanings of these words.

_____

_____

_____

_____

6. Can you think of any more homonyms? _____

_____

Write sentences using them.

IN YOUR WORDS

Write a few sentences to answer each of the following questions:

1. Write about your experience as a user of the World Wide Web. If you have no experience, write about what you think that the Web is like.

_____

_____

_____

_____

_____

2. What questions do you have about using the Web? Where could you go to get your questions answered?

_____

_____

_____

_____

3. What is your opinion of computers in general?

_____

_____

_____

_____

4. If you have a computer, write about it and how you use it.

_____

_____

_____

_____

SUMMING UP

1. Share answers to question 2 above. Compile a list of questions from number 2 for the class and share where you might get the answers.

2. Share answers to question 3 above. Write a summary statement of the opinion of the class about computers.

3. Remember your reading journal and vocabulary log.

REFLECTING AND SYNTHESIZING

A. Discuss your reading journal and vocabulary log with your partner or group. Have the exercises helped you answer all of your questions in your reading journal? Can you add any more words to your vocabulary log?

B. After answering the following, share your thoughts with your partner, group, or class:

1. A friend or relative from the same place that you came from is newly arrived in the United States. What advice would you give to him or her about shopping here?

2. In Chapter 3, the opening thought is "Hitch your wagon to a star." After reading Selection 2 in this chapter, do you still think that this old saying gives good advice? What would you add to this quotation?

3. How would you counsel a young person who said that his or her main goal in life is to get rich?

4. Do you like using a computer? Why or why not?

5. Has the material in this chapter changed your thinking? If yes, explain how it has changed.

C. Answer these questions on your own:

1. How does shopping in the United States differ from shopping where you came from?

2. Write about a good or bad experience that you had purchasing something.

3. Write about a good or bad experience that you had using a computer.

4. Write about your major and how you use or will use computers in it.

5. Write about what gives you happiness and contentment in your life.

6. What is your opinion of the thought that opened this chapter?

   Caveat emptor (Latin)—Let the buyer beware.

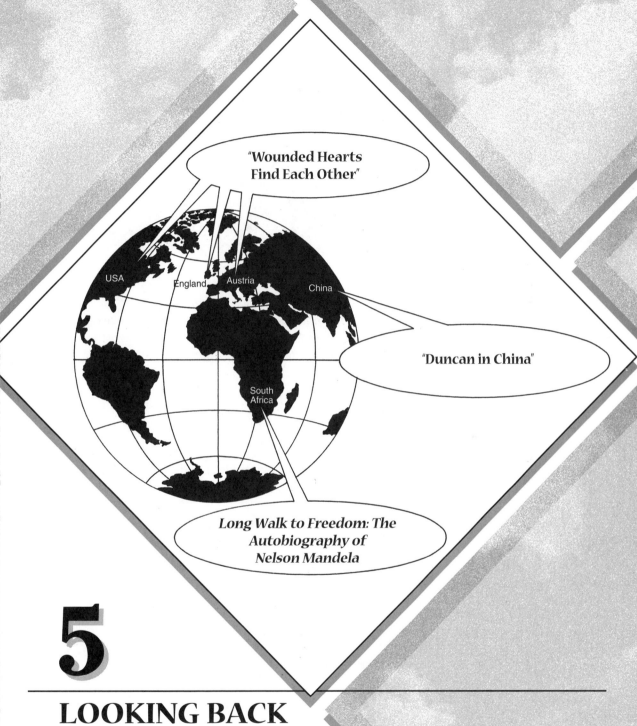

"Wounded Hearts Find Each Other"

USA   England   Austria   China

"Duncan in China"

South Africa

Long Walk to Freedom: The Autobiography of Nelson Mandela

5

LOOKING BACK

OPENING THOUGHT

Janus—from Roman mythology.
The god of gates and doorways and entrances and exits
with two faces looking in opposite directions.
One face looked into the past; the other into the future.

Take a few minutes to think about the Roman god that introduces this chapter. Answer the following questions:

1. For which month is Janus the symbol? _____

2. Do you think that Janus is a good symbol to introduce this chapter "Looking Back?" Why or why not?

   _____

   _____

3. Do you think that looking back is a good thing to do in life? Why or why not?

   _____

   _____

4. What are some events that people would look back at?

   _____

   _____

Share your thoughts with your partner, group, or class.

Selection 1

DISCOVER WHAT YOU KNOW

REMINDER:
Remember to preview the selections before you read. Also, make entries in your reading journal and vocabulary log as you read. In addition, remember to read for meaning, particularly the longer selections in this chapter.

If you don't know anything about the following, write "I don't know." If you have some ideas or questions about them, write these on the lines also.

1. What was the Holocaust?

_____

_____

_____

_____

2. What was Kristallnacht?

_____

_____

_____

_____

3. What do you know about the Kindertransport?

_____

_____

_____

_____

WOUNDED HEARTS FIND EACH OTHER

When Melissa Hacker was an elementary school girl growing up in New York City, she remembers feeling that her relationship with her mother, Ruth Morley, a successful costume designer for Hollywood films, was different from the relationships other children had with their parents.

5 "I grew up knowing there were things she was afraid of that had to do with her refugee experience," Ms. Hacker says. "Even when I was a little girl I would try to protect her from this big, bad, dangerous world. I felt that since so many scarier things had happened to her when she was my age than had happened to me, I shouldn't bother her with my little child's troubles."

10 It wasn't until many years later that Ms. Hacker, now 37, learned the full story of her mother's separation from her parents at the age of 13 in Vienna at the outset of the **Holocaust.** Ms. Morley, along with thousands of other Jewish children from Germany and Central Europe, was sent away to England where for the next year and a half she was shuttled among various

15 **foster** homes.

The story of Ms. Morley's emigration in January 1939 and its **reverberations** on Ms. Hacker's relationship

20 with her mother, who died of breast cancer in 1991, form the core of Ms. Hacker's **debut** documentary film, "My Knees Were Jumping:

25 Remembering the Kindertransports,". . . .

The Kindertransport is the name of the movement, organized by British Jews and

30 Quakers, to rescue some 10,000 mostly Jewish children from the **Nazis** in the nine months before the outbreak of World War II.

35 In Europe word spread quickly through the Jewish community that there was a rescue program for Jewish

Melissa Hacker, creator of a new documentary

children, most of whom ranged in age from 5 to 17. Parents would bring
their children to local Jewish community centers, where information and
photographs were collected and sent to committees in England. A few weeks
later transit papers would come back for some but not all of the children who
applied.

Usually the parents had only 24 hours to prepare their children and say
goodbye. Many of the trains left at night, and parents were not allowed on
the trains to see the trains off. The children were taken to the Netherlands,
then transferred to ferries that took them to Britain. Roughly 80 percent of
the children never saw their parents again. Ms. Morley was one of the lucky
ones. She was reunited with her parents in England a year and a half later,
and the family sailed to New York in the fall of 1940.

The **quirky** title of Ms. Hacker's documentary refers to an incident Ms.
Morley recounts in the film. On **Kristallnacht,** November 9, 1938, she was
hiding in a back room with her older half-sister, Lily, when Nazi officers
stormed into the apartment, smashed furniture and arrested her father, a
pharmacist. When Ms. Morley began to scream, Lily muffled her cries with
a pillow.

After being held in prison for 10 days, Ms. Morley's father was brought
home by two Nazi officers. Listening through the wall in the next room as
one of them telephoned headquarters to inquire whether they should leave
her father there or return him to prison, Ms. Morley fainted. In the film, she
recalls feeling as though her knees were jumping out of her skin. It was then
and there that her parents decided they had to get their child out of Austria.
. . .

Ms. Hacker had originally planned to make a movie about her
relationship with her mother (whose costume-design credits include "The
Miracle Worker," "Taxi Driver," "Annie Hall" and "The Prince of Tides")
and began interviewing her. As the details of Ms. Morley's childhood came
out, Ms. Hacker realized there was a larger story to tell. She did extensive
research at the Library of Congress and National Archives, where she
discovered one of the movie's most **haunting** film clips—a woman waving
goodbye—in the back of a file of Universal newsreels.

Her first major shoot was in the fall of 1990 at the first American
Kindertransport reunion in the Catskills. More than 300 people attended this
intensely emotional gathering, shown in the film, where Ms. Morley spoke
publicly for the first time about her childhood experiences.

Ms. Hacker, while filming, was moved to tears. "All around there were
people who hadn't seen each other in 50 years finding each other," she
recalls. "Many had brought their children and their grandchildren."

While Ms. Morley was in temporary **remission** from her cancer, she and her daughter traveled together to Vienna and visited the house where she had grown up. But because the Nazis didn't want the Kindertransport to be a public relations spectacle, the archival material in Vienna proved to be scarce.

Ms. Hacker, who studied film at New York University after attending Oberlin and the University of Washington, paid for the movie mostly from her earnings as an assistant film editor. The total cost was around $110,000, and it took her seven years to complete the film. Even before it was finished, she had begun to show it at Kindertransport reunion meetings as a work-in-progress.

In addition to looking at the lives of those who were saved by the Kindertransport movement, "My Knees Were Jumping" examines the complicated feelings of the next generation. Ms. Hacker was not alone in sensing a traumatic parental experience without ever being told exactly what had happened. Yet somehow the next generation knew. Ms. Hacker used to **brood about** what she would do if confined in a concentration camp, and her sister, Emily, who is two years younger, had nightmares about **storm troopers.**

Such anxieties, Ms. Hacker discovered, are shared by many of the second generation of the Kindertransport. She now belongs to a second-generation organization called KT2, which has about 200 members in the United States. They gather three times a year to share their experiences and have begun compiling a collection of videotaped oral histories as part of an archive.

Ms. Morley died before she could see her daughter's movie. But the making of the film had already made them closer. "It was wonderful to get it all out in the open and to share everything," Ms. Hacker says. "One thing I want the film to do is to open up communications in families. What has impressed me is the strength of the Kindertransport people and their ability to create new lives and new families. And I'm simply in **awe** of their parents, who had the strength to send their children away not knowing where they were going or what could happen to them."

Stephen Holden

Copyright © 1998 by the New York Times Company. Reprinted by permission.

GLOSSARY

awe (n.) a feeling of wonder and respect

brood about (v.) to think at length and unhappily about; worry about

debut (adj.) first

foster (adj.) giving parental care to somebody not legally related

haunting (adj.) coming again and again to the mind; unforgettable

Holocaust (n.) the mass killing of European Jews and others by the Nazis during World War II

Kristallnacht (n.) November 9, 1938. The Nazis attacked Jewish shops, businesses, and synagogues throughout Germany breaking many glass windows; hence, "Crystal night"

Nazi (n.) a member of the National Socialist German Workers' Party, founded in 1919 and brought to power by Adolf Hitler in 1933; (adj.) relating to Nazis

quirky (adj.) strange

remission (n.) the lessening of a disease

reverberation (n.) a repeated reflection

storm trooper (n.) a member of the Nazi militia noted for brutality and violence

QUICK COMPREHENSION CHECK

Complete the sentences with a word or phrase that fits in the blanks. Refer to the selection if you need to.

When Melissa Hacker was growing up she felt the relationship with

(1) _____ was **(2)** _____ than

other children had with their parents. She tried to **(3)** _____.

Many years later she learned that her mother was **(4)** _____

from her parents in January 1939 when she was 13 years old. Her mother was

part of the **(5)** _____ movement to rescue

(6) _____ children from the **(7)** _____.

Ms. Hacker made a **(8)** _____ called **(9)** _____

about her mother's experience and the effect it had on their relationship. She paid

for it mostly from **(10)** _____. She has shown it at

(11) _____. It tells the stories of the people and also helps

the (12) _____ understand their parents. Unfortunately,

Ms. Morley (13) _____ before it was completed.

However, the project had already (14) _____. Ms. Hacker

wants the film to (15) _____.

QUESTIONS FOR THOUGHT AND DISCUSSION

1. When Melissa Hacker was a little girl, what did she try to do for her mother? Why?

2. Years later, what did she learn had happened to her mother?

3. What was the Kindertransport movement? Why was it necessary?

4. What percent of the children saw their parents again?

5. What was Ms. Hacker's original plan for a movie? Why did she change her mind?

6. In addition to telling the stories of the people in the Kindertransport, what else did the film do?

7. What happened when Melissa and her mother went to Vienna?

8. What is KT2?

9. What effect did the film project have on the relationship between Ms. Hacker and her mother? What happened to her mother?

10. What impressed Ms. Hacker as she carried out her project?

ANOTHER LOOK AT THE SELECTION

You can do the following exercises in pairs or groups:

1. Since the documentary film is the subject of a large part of the article, putting the information about it in a chart is a useful way to absorb it.

MY KNEES WERE JUMPING: REMEMBERING
THE KINDERTRANSPORTS

  a. FILMMAKER
  Who is the maker of the film?

b. TITLE
Where did the title come from?

_____

c. IDEA FOR THE MOVIE
Where did the filmmaker get the idea for the movie?

_____

d. COST
How much?
Where did she get the money?

_____

e. LENGTH OF TIME TO MAKE THE MOVIE
How much time?

_____

f. RESEARCH FOR THE FILM
How many types of research?
Description of each type:

_____

g. QUALIFICATIONS OF THE FILMMAKER
What training did Melissa Hacker have?

_____

2. The information about the film in the article is presented above. What else would you like to know about this film? List your questions below. How could you find the answers to your questions?

_____

_____

_____

_____

_____

_____

VOCABULARY BUILDING

> **VOCABULARY STRATEGIES:**
> To summarize, there are a number of strategies to apply when trying to figure out the meaning of a word.
>
> 1. Decide whether the word is a **key** word, that is, whether it is essential to understanding the meaning of the reading. If the word is a key word, you will need to know its meaning. If not, you may choose whether or not to find out its meaning.
>
> 2. Try to get the meaning from context, the words and sentences around the vocabulary word.
>
> 3. Use your knowledge of common prefixes and suffixes to figure out the meanings of words.
>
> 4. Use your knowledge of the parts of speech to help you find out the meanings of words.
>
> 5. It is possible to use more than one strategy to determine the meaning of a word or phrase.
>
> 6. If, after using the strategies, you still do not know the meaning of the word, you will have to look it up in the dictionary. Make sure that you choose the correct meaning from the dictionary entry for the particular context you are working on.

Exercise 1: In the following sentences identify which strategy (or strategies) you use to determine the meaning of the vocabulary in **bold print.** The strategies are determining the meaning from context, prefixes and suffixes, and parts of speech. The first one has been done as an example.

1. The **Kindertransport** is the name of the movement, organized by British Jews and Quakers, to rescue some 10,000 mostly Jewish children from the Nazis in the nine months before the outbreak of World War II.

   Meaning of the word *the moving or transporting of children to save them from the Nazis*

   Strategy or strategies used *context; part of speech*

2. She was **reunited** with her parents in England a year and a half later, and the family sailed to New York in the fall of 1940.

   Meaning of the word _____

   Strategy or strategies used _____

   _____

3. Her first major **shoot** was in the fall of 1990 at the first American Kindertransport reunion in the Catskills.

   Meaning of the word _____

   Strategy or strategies used _____

   _____

4. Ms. Hacker was not alone in sensing a **traumatic** parental experience without ever being told exactly had happened.

   Meaning of the word _____

   Strategy or strategies used _____

   _____

5. Ms. Hacker was not alone in sensing a traumatic **parental** experience without ever being told exactly what had happened.

   Meaning of the word _____

   Strategy or strategies used _____

   _____

6. But because the Nazis didn't want the Kindertransport to be a public relations spectacle, the **archival** material in Vienna proved to be scarce.

   Meaning of the word _____

   _____

   Strategy or strategies used _____

   _____

7. They gather three times a year to share their experiences and have begun compiling a collection of videotaped oral histories as part of an **archive.**

   Meaning of the word _____

   _____

   Strategy or strategies used _____

   _____

Exercise 2: In the film Ms. Morley, Melissa Hacker's mother, tells what happened on Kristallnacht.

> . . . On Kristallnacht, November 9, 1938, she (Ms. Morley) was hiding in a back room with her older half-sister, Lily, when Nazi officers stormed into the apartment, smashed furniture and arrested her father, a pharmacist. When Ms. Morley began to scream, Lily muffled her cries with a pillow.
>
> After being held in prison for 10 days, Ms. Morley's father was brought home by two Nazi officers. Listening through the wall in the next room as one of them telephoned headquarters to inquire whether they should leave her father there or return him to prison, Ms. Morley fainted. In the film, she recalls feeling as though her knees were jumping out of her skin. It was then and there that her parents decided they had to get their child out of Austria.

1. Circle the words or phrases that make you see and feel what is happening. Enter in your vocabulary log any words that are new for you.

_____

2. What is the word picture that Ms. Morley uses to describe her fright?

_____

3. Write two word pictures to describe fright.

_____

_____

IN YOUR WORDS

Write a few sentences to answer each of the following questions:

1. Why do you think that Ms. Morley could not talk to her young daughter about her experiences in the Kindertransport movement?

_____

_____

_____

2. Do you think that the film could open up communication in families? Why or why not?

_____

_____

_____

_____

3. Which part of the article impressed you most? Why?

_____

_____

_____

_____

4. Write about something frightening that you experienced. Use a word picture to describe your fright.

_____

_____

_____

_____

SUMMING UP

1. Write a summary paragraph of what you know about the film "My Knees Were Jumping: Remembering the Kindertransports." Identify the film and the filmmaker in the first sentence. Use the information from number 1 in Another Look at the Selection.

   The documentary film "My Knees Were Jumping: Remembering the Kindertransports" by _____

   _____

   _____

   _____

   _____

   _____

   _____

   _____

   _____

2. Exchange your summary with a partner or group member. Answer the following questions while reading your partner's summary:

   A. Is all the important information about the film included in the summary? If not, what is missing?

   B. Are the sentences clear? If not, which ones are not clear?

   C. Are there any suggestions that you can make about the summary paragraph?

3. When you receive your summary paragraph back from your partner, make another copy of it including any changes that you wish to make based on your partner's comments.

4. Remember your reading journal and vocabulary log.

Selection 2

DISCOVER WHAT YOU THINK

1. How can living in a different place change a person's life?

_____

_____

2. How can living in a different place change a person's thinking?

_____

_____

3. Freewrite about yourself, a family member, or someone you know and the experience of living in a different place. Continue until your teacher tells you to stop.

FROM "DUNCAN IN CHINA"

Duncan Hsu, foreign expert. That was his name in China. In America, it had been Duncan Hsu, dropout. He had dropped out of a military academy, a law school, a computer-programming night class, a ten-year-old **soap opera** of a relationship, and even, recently, out of a career-exploration minicourse.

5 As a result, he was now thirty-seven, with many people not speaking to him—for example, his mother and, so far as he could tell, his father. His father was a master of the art of speechifying without speaking, unlike Duncan's mother, who called every day, **lest** Duncan forget she was not speaking to him. She called lest he imagine he had become the sort of son

10 about whom she could boast, or lest he overlook how well his brother Arnie was doing. Arnie had started an import-export business, which now employed sixteen lucky people. Arnie drove a BMW convertible and wore wraparound sunglasses. Arnie had his car washed inside and out while he went shopping with his girlfriend from Hong Kong. Arnie was at one with

15 the Chinese **bourgeois** experience.

Duncan, on the other hand, tortured himself with the idea that there had to be more to his heritage. He went to China because, having seen **Sung dynasty porcelains** in museums, he wanted to know more about that China—the China of the scholar-officials, the China of **ineffable** nobility

20 and restraint. Duncan was no artist—art school was the one kind of school

he had never thought to drop out of. But those porcelains could make him cry, what with their grace and purity, and delicate **crackle glazes;** what with their wholeness and confidence and supremely untortured air. They made him feel what life could be, and what his life was. They were uplifting; they were depressing. That was beauty for you. Duncan had not been an Asian anything major, but in his frequent periods of **incipient** employment, he had read about the tremendous integrity of the Sung scholar-officials, and had speculated that some of their noble code had survived in the spirit of the **Long**

Sung Stoneware

March. Should there not be, somewhere, an **iota** of it left still? Maybe even in his own family? He had had scholars in his family, after all; they had not always been attitudinal geniuses of his brother's **ilk.** Some of them had run schools. One of his father's brothers had been a kind of horticulturist-folklorist-herbalist; he married a violinist-entomologist. Their son, Duncan's cousin, was still alive and living in China. Perhaps Duncan would have a chance to meet him.

Or perhaps Duncan would fall in love. Later, Duncan would remember that even before he left the United States, even before he met the perhaps beautiful, perhaps noble, completely maddening Louise, he had considered the possibility of love. For wasn't that what happened to people in foreign lands? He'd learned that from the movies. Anything was possible. So argued one voice in his head, even as another said, **Folly.**

Folly. Almost as soon as Duncan reached Shandong, he knew that he had come for **naught,** that the China of the early 1980s had more to do with eating melon seeds around a coal heater the size of a bread box than about Sung dynasty porcelain. He gave up his goal easily, more easily than he would have thought possible. He flowed, a man without dismay, and all on account of the cold. At home he had **railed against** degree programs, movies, voting procedures, sports equipment. He had **reviled** the local Motor Vehicle Department; he had denounced mindlessness, fecklessness, spinelessness. But in China so many things were poorly run and poorly designed that there was no point in railing against them. And who could fault the people for a certain **scrappy** element? Certainly not in the winter. Duncan had read tableloads of books about China before he left, but none had prepared him for the **plunge** in mental functioning that he experienced; it was as if his thoughtbearing fluids had gone **viscous.** There were two kinds of rooms for him now—barely heated, and unheated. There were two kinds of days—slightly warmer, and no warmer. When Duncan had a chance to catch a reflection of himself, he was amazed to see how much less baby-faced he looked here than at home. His face was no gaunter, and still featured dimples, but it was chapped and reddened in a cowboy-on-the-prairie kind of way, rather than smooth and shiny enough to be featured in a soap ad. This brought him a certain, specific contentment. More generally, though, he was contented when he was warm enough, and discontented when he was not. Whereas at home he had been impatient with people who thought of nothing but their comfort, now he thought of nothing but his comfort.

Already, in short, Duncan was becoming like Professor Mo, the head of the English-language program at the coal mining institute to which Duncan was assigned. Professor Mo always made sure that Duncan the foreign expert was seated next to whatever **meager** heat source might be available, if only so that he, as protector and guide of the foreign expert, might also sit next to the meager heat source.

. . .

Finally, finally it was getting to be spring. That meant, first of all, that instead of winter cabbage, day in and day out, now there were other vegetables to eat—first big scallions, then spinach and leeks, then small scallions. The trees began to green, beginning with the willows, bringing shade. Quilts were hung out to air. Students went for walks. Often Duncan would glimpse Louise's small, slim figure out with one classmate or another; she seemed to pick a different classmate every day. People began to play basketball on the packed dirt court outside Duncan's window. As often as he could, Duncan joined them. This brought him real pleasure, especially the couple of times Louise managed to goad some of the other women into playing with the guys. How startlingly quick and savvy she was! **Agile** as a greyhound, she was able to find her merry way around players far bigger and younger than she, including Duncan. Every day he hoped she would be moved to play again.

In the meantime, a fish truck came. For an hour, a man with red gloves stood astride a mountain of ice and shoveled fish out into the baskets borne by the joyful crowd. Fish and fish parts rained through the air as if it were New Year's; the silver scales threw out points of light. People feasted. Duncan began to shed layers of clothes. By now he was beginning to feel more at home speaking Chinese, and could at least answer the kinds of questions people typically asked him—had he eaten yet, and did he like salty food or sweet, and was a place clean or dirty. He could buy stamps at the post office; he could bargain over what little there was for sale. Also, he had

begun to feel more at home in his apartment, which featured a concrete floor
and a **hodgepodge** of furniture, ranging from an enormous, Art Deco
wardrobe with veined mirrors to a blue metal bedstand, spray-painted with
panda bears. There was a coal stove, which had not quite warmed the room
in the winter but did now; and to go with it, a maid, Mrs. Su, whose job it
was to keep after the coal soot that seemed to settle everywhere.

. . .

. . . As the weeks went on, Duncan spent more and more time with his
students. He made dumplings with them. He watched TV with them, helping
them translate endless, plodding programs about **Buckingham Palace.** He
discussed world affairs with them. He visited their dorms.

And, best of all, he went on excursions with them, in the ancient, green
car he shared with the school leaders. . . . The driver had once proudly
shown Duncan how he had painstakingly fashioned his own replacement
springs from heavy-gauge wire.

If only Duncan enjoyed as much control over the contents of the car! Not
that Professor Mo proved his inescapable guide on every trip. But Mo took
Duncan to task for choosing William [one of Duncan's students; they had
chosen English names] instead of himself for an excursion to **Confucius's**
gravesite at Qufu. And regarding Duncan's plan to take Louise with him to
climb the holy Buddhist mountain, Tai Shan—did he really think it
appropriate to take a woman, alone, with him anywhere?

"I put her name down on the schedule for a turn but meant for her to
bring a partner," sighed Duncan—who in truth had half-dreamed some
oversight might occur. "Besides, there would have, of course, been the
driver."

"May I name myself to be that partner?" said Mo.

"Oh no, no, you are far too busy with important matters," protested
Duncan.

"In other words," said Mo, "you would prefer not to have a lightbulb."

Duncan started a little; "lightbulb" was the same term his father used for
a chaperone. "You're welcome to come, Professor Mo, but I understand it's
quite a climb. I'm not sure I'll make it myself. Haven't you had an operation
on your lung? Certainly there will be other opportunities . . ."

Professor Mo studied him openly, smoking. He was wearing a three-
piece suit today, the vest of which sported several moth holes. "Of course,
you are single man," he said.

"I have a girlfriend," lied Duncan, even as Louise's **visage** floated before
him, complete with cupped chin.

"Perhaps I will accompany you to the mountain base," said Mo. "And
then, of course, there is the other excursion."

"What other excursion?"

145 "To see your relatives."

"Has that been approved?" Duncan had succeeded in contacting his cousin's family by mail a few months before, but had been seeking permission from the provincial and school officials for a visit ever since.

Mo nodded.

150 "And they have permission, too?"

"Their unit wants them to travel down from Harbin to Beijing, to meet you. That way you will not see their living conditions."

"How typical—wonderful!" said Duncan. "Thank you for your help in arranging this. It was kind of you." He blurted out this last without sarcasm.

155 "I have not been to Beijing in some years," observed Professor Mo. "It will be pleasant to visit, especially in the spring." He snuffed out his cigarette, then hooked his thumbs in his vest, arms **akimbo.**

. . .

From *Who's Irish?* by Gish Jen. Copyright © 1999 by Gish Jen. Reprinted by permission of Alfred A. Knopf, a Division of Random House, Inc.

GLOSSARY

agile (adj.) physically able to move quickly

akimbo (adj.) with the hands on hips and the elbows bowed outward

bourgeois (adj.) middle class

Buckingham Palace (name) residence of the Queen of England in London

Confucius (name) Chinese philosopher and teacher (557?–479 B.C.) His teachings emphasized devotion to parents, family, and friends, ancestor worship, and the maintenance of justice and peace.

crackle glaze (n.) a coating with cracks in it covering porcelain

folly (n.) a foolish idea

hodgepodge (n.) a mixture of various things; a jumble

ilk (n.) type or kind

incipient (n.) beginning to exist or appear

ineffable (n.) indescribable

iota (n.) a very small amount

lest (conj.) for fear that

Long March (name) a retreat of the Chinese Red Army (Communist) during the civil war in China in the 1930s. It was a significant event in the Chinese Communist movement.

meager (adj.) small in quantity

naught (n.) nothing

plunge (n.) steep or sharp fall

rail against (v.) to criticize in bitter, harsh, or abusive language

revile (v.) to criticize someone or something with abusive language

scrappy (adj.) quarrelsome

soap opera (n.) a drama, typically performed as a serial on daytime television, showing daily life and melodrama

Sung dynasty porcelain (n.) from the Chinese dynasty (960–1279) that was marked by cultural advance and prosperity

visage (n.) face

viscous (adj.) having relatively high resistance to flow; thick, sticky

QUICK COMPREHENSION CHECK ☑

Complete the sentences with a word or phrase that fits in the blanks. Refer to the selection if you need to.

Duncan Hsu's life in the United States was **(1)** _____.

He decided to go to **(2)** _____. One thing that

motivated him to go was **(3)** _____. When he arrived, he

(4) _____. He had a job in a **(5)** _____

and was called **(6)** _____. Professor Mo was

(7) _____. Louise was **(8)** _____ there.

Duncan wanted to take a **(9)** _____ with Louise, but

Professor Mo **(10)** _____. Professor Mo said that he would

(11) _____. Professor Mo also told Duncan that the trip to

(12) _____ was approved by the officials. He said that he

and Duncan would travel together to see **(13)** _____.

QUESTIONS FOR THOUGHT AND DISCUSSION

1. What did Duncan Hsu's mother and father think of him?
2. Why did they think this way?
3. What did Duncan decide to do?
4. What motivated him to do this?
5. What did Duncan think when he arrived in Shandong?
6. What was Duncan's job?
7. What was Professor Mo's job?
8. Who was Louise and how did he feel about her?
9. What did Duncan like best about his duties?
10. What did Professor Mo say about the two excursions discussed? Why do you think that he said this?

ANOTHER LOOK AT THE SELECTION

You can do the following exercises in pairs or groups:

1. The selection makes contrasts. One example is the picture presented of Duncan and his brother Arnie.

Duncan	
	1. He was a dropout from schools and courses.
	2. He dropped out of a relationship of ten years.
	3. His father was angry with him and was not speaking to him.
	4. His mother was angry with him and was speaking to him.
	5. He did not hold a steady job.

Arnie	
	1. He was doing very well.
	2. His mother was proud of him.
	3. He started an export-import business that employed 16 people.
	4. He drove a BMW convertible.
	5. He had a girlfriend from Hong Kong.

Summary statement: The selection presents Duncan and Arnie as opposites: Arnie is successful while Duncan is not.

Now contrast the way Duncan was before his stay in China and the way he is while in China. List details presented in the selection to show the contrast. Make a statement that summarizes the contrast as shown above.

Duncan before China

_____

_____

_____

Duncan in China

_____

_____

_____

Summary statement: _____

_____

2. Read the dialogue in the selection again between Duncan and Professor Mo. Continue it by writing several more exchanges between the two men.

VOCABULARY BUILDING

Exercise 1: In the following sentences identify which strategy (or strategies) you use to determine the meaning of the vocabulary in **bold print.** The strategies are determining the meaning from context, prefixes and suffixes, and parts of speech.

1. His father was a master of the art of **speechifying** without speaking, unlike Duncan's mother, who called every day, lest Duncan forget she was not speaking to him.

   Meaning of the word _____

   Strategy or strategies used _____

2. He had reviled the local Motor Vehicle Department; he had denounced **mindlessness, fecklessness, spinelessness.**

   Meaning of the word _____

   Strategy or strategies used _____

3. More generally, though, he was contented when he was warm enough, and **discontented** when he was not.

   Meaning of the word _____

   Strategy or strategies used _____

4. People began to play basketball on the packed dirt court outside Duncan's window. As often as he could, Duncan joined them. This brought him real pleasure, especially the couple of times Louise managed to **goad** some of the other women into playing with the guys.

   Meaning of the word _____

   Strategy or strategies used _____

5. In the meantime, a fish truck came. For an hour, a man with red gloves stood **astride** a mountain of ice and shoveled fish out into the baskets borne by the joyful crowd.

   Meaning of the word _____

   Strategy or strategies used _____

6. "May I name myself to be that partner?" said Mo.
   "Oh no, no, you are far too busy with important matters," protested Duncan.
   "In other words," said Mo, "you would prefer not to have a **lightbulb.**"
   Duncan started a little; "**lightbulb**" was the same term his father used for a chaperone.

   Meaning of the word _____

   Strategy or strategies used _____

7. "Perhaps I will accompany you to the mountain base," said Mo. "And then, of course, there is the other **excursion.**"
    "What other **excursion?**"
    "To see your relatives."
    "Has that been approved?" Duncan had succeeded in contacting his cousin's family by mail a few months before, but had been seeking permission from the provincial and school officials for a visit ever since.

    Meaning of the word _____

    Strategy or strategies used _____

Exercise 2: Descriptions with details are important in this selection. Details give the reader the picture that the author has in her or his mind. One example is the description of spring. List the details about spring that the author gives. Enter any new vocabulary in your vocabulary log.

_____

_____

_____

Exercise 3: Choose another description that you like from the selection and list the details that the author gives to draw the picture. Enter any new vocabulary in your vocabulary log.

_____

_____

_____

IN YOUR WORDS

Write answers to the following:

1. What do you think is going to happen?

    To Duncan when he meets his relatives in Beijing?

_____

_____

_____

To Duncan and Louise?

_____

_____

_____

To Duncan in the future?

_____

_____

_____

2. Based on what you have read, describe the kind of man that you think Duncan Hsu is.

_____

_____

3. Choose a season that you like. Write a description including details that make a picture for the reader.

_____

_____

_____

_____

_____

SUMMING UP

1. In pairs or groups share your answers to number 1 in In Your Words.

2. Choose the answers your pair or group likes best and together write an ending to the excerpt from _Duncan in China._

3. Share your ending with the rest of the class. The class can then vote to choose which one the members like best.

4. Remember your reading journal and vocabulary log.

Selection 3

DISCOVER WHAT YOU KNOW

What do you know about Nelson Mandela? Write down some things that you know about him. If you don't know anything, write "I don't know anything." If there is information that you would like to know, write that below, too.

_____

_____

_____

_____

FROM *LONG WALK TO FREEDOM:* *THE AUTOBIOGRAPHY OF NELSON MANDELA*

From "A Country Childhood"

The village of Qunu was situated in a narrow, grassy valley crisscrossed by clear streams, and overlooked by green hills. It consisted of no more than a few hundred people who lived in huts, which were beehive-shaped structures of mud walls, with a wooden pole in the center holding up a

5 peaked, grass roof. The floor was made of crushed ant-heap, the hard dome of excavated earth above an ant colony, and was kept smooth by smearing regularly with cow **dung.** The smoke from the hearth escaped through the roof, and the only opening was a low doorway one had to **stoop** to walk through. The huts were generally grouped together in a residential area that

10 was some distance away from the **maize** fields. There were no roads, only paths through the grass worn away by barefooted boys and women. The women and children of the village wore blankets dyed in **ocher**; only the few Christians in the village wore Western-style clothing. Cattle, sheep, goats, and horses grazed together in common pastures. The land around

15 Qunu was mostly treeless except for a cluster of poplars on a hill overlooking the village. The land itself was owned by the state. With very few exceptions, Africans at the time did not enjoy private title to land in South Africa but were tenants paying rent annually to the government. In the area, there were two small primary schools, a general store, and a dipping

20 tank to rid the cattle of ticks and diseases.

. . .

My mother **presided** over three huts at Qunu which, as I remember, were always filled with the babies and children of my relations. In fact, I hardly recall any occasion as a child when I was alone. In African culture, the sons and daughters of one's aunts or uncles are considered brothers and sisters, not cousins. We do not make the same distinctions among relations practiced by whites. We have no half brothers or half sisters. My mother's sister is my mother; my uncle's son is my brother; my brother's child is my son, my daughter.

. . .

From an early age, I spent most of my free time in the **veld** playing and fighting with the other boys in the village. A boy who remained at home tied to his mother's apron strings was regarded as a sissy. At night, I shared my food and blanket with these same boys. I was no more than five when I became a herd-boy, looking after sheep and calves in the fields. I discovered the almost **mystical** attachment that the **Xhosa** have for cattle, not only as a source of food and wealth, but as a blessing from God and a source of

happiness. It was in the fields that I learned how to knock birds out of the
sky with a slingshot, to gather wild honey and fruits and edible roots, to
swim in the clear, cold streams, and to catch fish with **twine** and sharpened
bits of wire. I learned to stick-fight—essential knowledge to any rural

40   African boy—and became adept at its various techniques, parrying blows,
feinting in one direction and striking in another, breaking away from an
opponent with quick footwork. From these days I date my love of the veld,
of open spaces, the simple beauties of nature, the clean line of the horizon.
. . .

One night, when I was nine years old, I was aware of a **commotion** in the

45   household. My father, who took turns visiting his wives and usually came to
us for perhaps one week a month, had arrived. But it was not at his
accustomed time, for he was not scheduled to be with us for another few
days. I found him in my mother's hut, lying on his back on the floor, in the
midst of what seemed like an endless fit of coughing. Even to my young

50   eyes, it was clear that my father was not long for this world. . . . My father
smoked and became calm. He continued smoking for perhaps an hour, and
then, his pipe still lit, he died.

I do not remember experiencing great grief so much as feeling cut **adrift.**
Although my mother was the center of my existence, I defined myself

55   through my father. My father's passing changed my whole life in a way that
I did not suspect at the time. After a brief period of mourning, my mother
informed me that I would be leaving Qunu. I did not ask her why, or where I
was going.

I packed the few things that I possessed, and early one morning we set

60   out on a journey westward to my new residence. I mourned less for my
father than for the world I was leaving behind. Qunu was all that I knew, and
I loved it in the unconditional way that a child loves his first home. Before
we disappeared behind the hills, I turned and looked for what I imagined
was the last time at my village. . . . Above all else, my eyes rested on the

65   three simple huts where I had enjoyed my mother's love and protection. It
was these three huts that I associated with all my happiness, with life itself,
and I **rued** the fact that I had not kissed each of them before I left. I could
not imagine that the future I was walking toward could compare in any way
to the past that I was leaving behind.

From "Rivonia"

70   . . . I had been reading my speech, and at this point I placed my papers on
the defense table, and turned to face the judge. The courtroom became
extremely quiet. I did not take my eyes off Justice de Wet as I spoke from
memory the final words.

75　During my lifetime I have dedicated myself to this struggle of the African people. I have fought against white domination, and I have fought against black domination. I have **cherished** the ideal of a democratic and free society in which all persons live together in harmony and with equal opportunities. It is an ideal which I hope to live for and to achieve. But if needs be, it is an ideal for which I am prepared to die. . . .

From "Freedom"

80　. . . It was during those long and lonely years [in prison] that my hunger for the freedom of my own people became a hunger for the freedom of all people, white and black. I knew as well as I knew anything that the oppressor must be liberated just as surely as the oppressed. A man who takes away another man's freedom is a prisoner of hatred, he is locked behind the **85** bars of prejudice and narrow-mindedness. I am not truly free if I am taking away someone else's freedom, just as surely as I am not free when my freedom is taken from me. The oppressed and the oppressor alike are robbed of their humanity.

　When I walked out of prison, that was my mission, to **liberate** the **90** oppressed and oppressor both. Some say that has now been achieved. But I know that that is not the case. The truth is that we are not yet free; we have

Nelson Mandela in his cell at Robben Island Prison, South Africa.
He spent eighteen of his seventy-seven years in prison in this cell.

merely achieved the freedom to be free, the right not to be oppressed. We have not taken the final step of our journey, but the first step on a longer and even more difficult road. For to be free is not merely to cast off one's chains, but to live in a way that respects and enhances the freedom of others. The true test of our **devotion** to freedom is just beginning.

I have walked that long road to freedom. I have tried not to **falter;** I have made missteps along the way. But I have discovered the secret that after climbing a great hill, one only finds that there are many more hills to climb. I have taken a moment here to rest, to **steal** a view of the glorious **vista** that surrounds me, to look back on the distance I have come. But I can rest only for a moment, for with freedom come responsibilities and I dare not **linger,** for my long walk is not yet ended.

From *The Long Walk to Freedom* by Nelson Mandela. Copyright © 1994 by Nelson Rolihlahla Mandela. By permission of Little, Brown and Company (Inc.).

GLOSSARY

adrift (adv.) without direction or purpose

cherish (v.) to regard something with appreciation; value highly

commotion (n.) a disturbance or confusion

devotion (n.) dedication

dung (n.) manure

falter (v.) lose confidence, strength, or purpose

feint (v.) to make a movement that is meant to deceive by diverting attention from the real target

liberate (v.) to set free from confinement or control

linger (v.) to be slow in leaving

maize (n.) corn

mystical (adj.) based on spiritual understanding rather than experience or reason

ocher (adj.) yellowish or brownish orange color

preside (v.) to hold the position of authority

Rivonia (n. adj.) Rivonia Trial: The State versus Nelson Mandela in which he was charged with trying to overthrow the government by force. The maximum penalty for the charge was death by hanging. Mandela spoke as a witness during the trial. His sentence was life in prison.

rue (v.) to feel regret or sorrow for something

steal (v.) to enjoy something secretly

stoop (v.) to bend (the head and body) forward and down

twine (n.) strong cord or string

veld (n.) any of the open grazing areas of southern Africa

vista (n.) distant view

Xhosa (name) members of a Bantu people living in the eastern part of Cape Province, South Africa

QUICK COMPREHENSION CHECK

Complete the sentences with a word or phrase that fits in the blanks. Refer to the selection if you need to.

In "A Country Childhood" Nelson Mandela describes **(1)** _____ in the village of Qunu. He describes the **(2)** _____ where people lived and the **(3)** _____ that they wore. He also describes the **(4)** _____ around Qunu. His mother had **(5)** _____ which were always filled with **(6)** _____. He also describes the **(7)** _____ that he did as a boy. At age nine, his father **(8)** _____. After a short period, he and his mother **(9)** _____. Nelson Mandela **(10)** _____ Qunu. "Rivonia" takes place in a **(11)** _____ during Mandela's **(12)** _____. In his speech Mandela states that he has cherished the ideal of a **(13)** _____. He states that he **(14)** _____ for his ideal. In "Freedom" Mandela says that there must be freedom for both **(15)** _____ and **(16)** _____. He says that the test of devotion to **(17)** _____ is just beginning. Finally, he says that he has **(18)** _____ the long road to **(19)** _____, has stopped a moment to **(20)** _____ but must not **(21)** _____ because **(22)** _____.

QUESTIONS FOR THOUGHT AND DISCUSSION

"A Country Childhood"

A. Write *T* for true or *F* for false.

_____ **1.** Qunu was a large village of 1,000 people.

_____ **2.** The houses in the village were made of mud with grass roofs.

_____ **3.** A dirt road led from the nearest town to the village.

_____ **4.** The Mandela family owned land in Qunu.

_____ **5.** Nelson Mandela's mother had three huts in the village.

_____ **6.** Nelson was often alone in the hut.

_____ **7.** Nelson spent most of his free time in his mother's hut.

_____ **8.** Nelson is a member of the Xhosa ethnic group.

_____ **9.** Nelson's father died when he was 21 years of age.

_____ **10.** Nelson felt happy when he left Qunu for the first time.

B. Answer the following in sentences:

"A Country Childhood"

1. How did Nelson Mandela feel about his life in Qunu?

2. What was his relationship with his mother?

3. What was his relationship with his father?

"Rivonia"

1. Under what circumstances was Nelson Mandela giving this speech?

2. To what did he dedicate himself during his lifetime?

3. What did he fight against?

4. In your own words, state Nelson Mandela's ideal.

"Freedom"

1. What does Mandela think about the oppressor?

2. What does he think about the oppressed?

3. What was his mission when he left prison?

4. Does he feel that his mission has been completely achieved? Why or why not?

5. What did Mandela discover on his long walk to freedom?

6. Does Mandela consider his long walk finished? Support your answer from the text.

ANOTHER LOOK AT THE SELECTION

You can do the following exercises in pairs or groups:

1. Mandela's description of Qunu is effective because of the details that he gives. List at least eight of these details on the following lines. Enter new vocabulary in your vocabulary log.

_____

_____

2. List the details that Mandela gives to help the reader understand African family life. Enter new vocabulary in your vocabulary log.

_____

_____

3. What is your opinion of Mandela's ideal as stated in the excerpt from "Rivonia"? What do you think of his statement that he would die for it?

_____

_____

VOCABULARY BUILDING

Exercise 1: Choose five words from this selection and tell which vocabulary strategies helped you figure out their meaning. The vocabulary strategies are determining the meaning from context, prefixes and suffixes, and parts of speech. Fill out the following for each word. Enter the words in your vocabulary log.

Sentence where the word is found _____

_____

Meaning of the word _____

_____

Strategy or strategies used _____

_____

Exercise 2: In the last part of the selection, Mandela calls his life's journey a long walk to freedom. In the paragraph below, underline the details that create the picture of this walk. Use vocabulary strategies to find the meanings of words that you do not know.

> I have walked that long road to freedom. I have tried not to falter; I have made missteps along the way. But I have discovered the secret that after climbing a great hill, one only finds that there are many more hills to climb. I have taken a moment here to rest, to steal a view of the glorious vista that surrounds me, to look back on the distance I have come. But I can rest only for a moment, for with freedom come responsibilities, and I dare not linger, for my long walk is not yet ended.

Exercise 3: With the class make a list of other things that a life's journey might be called.

IN YOUR WORDS

Write your answers to the following questions:

1. Choose one phrase from the list in Exercise 3 above and write about your life. Include as many details as you can.

_____

_____

_____

_____

_____

2. What is your opinion of Nelson Mandela based on the selection?

_____

_____

_____

_____

_____

3. What else would you like to know about Mandela?

_____

_____

_____

_____

_____

4. Where could you go to find the answers to your questions?

_____

_____

_____

_____

_____

SUMMING UP

Share your answers to the following:

1. Which sentence in the selection summarizes Mandela's feeling for his country childhood?

2. Write a sentence that summarizes your feeling about your childhood.

3. Which paragraph summarizes Mandela's life at the writing of this autobiography?

4. What happened to Mandela after he wrote _Long Walk to Freedom_?

5. Where is Nelson Mandela now?

6. Compare your opinion of Nelson Mandela with opinions of members of your class. Do you all agree? Write a summary statement of what the class thinks of Nelson Mandela.

7. Did the class exercises help you answer your questions in your reading journal? Have you made your entries in your vocabulary log?

REFLECTING AND SYNTHESIZING

A. Discuss your vocabulary log and reading journal with the class.

1. How did the log and journal help you?

2. What suggestions can you make about how to do them?

B. After answering the following, share your thoughts with your partner, group, or class:

1. Which selection did you like the best? Why?

2. Are there any similarities among the three selections? If "Yes," what are they?

3. Are there any differences among the three selections? If "Yes," what are they?

4. Which selection would you like to learn more about? What could you do to learn more about it?

5. How does the picture of the Roman god Janus at the beginning of the chapter relate to each of the selections?

C. Answer these on your own:

1. Describe a documentary film that you would like to make about your family.

2. Write about when you had to leave someone that you loved.

3. Do you think that a person remains the same after living for a period of time in another country? Why or why not? If not, write about how a person could change as a result of the experience.

4. Write about things in the United States that impressed you when you first arrived.

5. Write about things in the United States that you did not like when you arrived.

6. Write about leaving a place that you love. Include things that you miss about that special place.

7. Write about family life in your culture.

8. Write a paragraph summarizing where you are in your life at this time.

9. Do you think people should look back? Why or why not?

10. Look back in writing at an event from your life.